Learning Couchbase

Design documents and implement real-world
e-commerce applications with Couchbase

Henry Potsangbam

[PACKT] open source*

PUBLISHING   community experience distilled

BIRMINGHAM - MUMBAI

Learning Couchbase

First published: November 2015

Production reference: 1171115

Published by Packt Publishing Ltd.
Livery Place
35 Livery Street
Birmingham B3 2PB, UK.

ISBN 978-1-78528-859-3

www.packtpub.com

Credits

Author
Henry Potsangbam

Reviewers
Tigran Babloyan
Clive Holloway
Marcus Johansson

Commissioning Editor
Neil Alexander

Acquisition Editor
Nikhil Karkal

Content Development Editor
Samantha Gonsalves

Technical Editor
Deepti Tuscano

Copy Editors
Merilyn Pereira
Vikrant Phadke

Project Coordinator
Kinjal Bari

Proofreader
Safis Editing

Indexer
Rekha Nair

Production Coordinator
Manu Joseph

Cover Work
Manu Joseph

About the Author

Henry Potsangbam is an experienced software developer, administrator, and architect with more than 14 years of experience in enterprise application architecture, design, and development. He's worked in various dómains, such as e-commerce, retail, and energy sectors. He is an IBM certified application and solution developer, SAP Certified Netweaver EP Consultant and CIPM (project management).

Always fascinated by and interested in exploring emerging technologies to solve business scenarios, Henry has been following NoSQL and Couchbase since its initial release around 2011.

In his spare time, he explores, and educates professionals in big data technologies such as Hadoop (Mapr, Hortonworks, and Cloudera), enterprise integration (camel, fuse esb, and Mule), analytics with R, messaging with kafka, rabbitMQ, the OSGI framework, NoSQL (Couchbase, Cassandra, and Mongodb), enterprise architecture, and so on. During his career, he architect private cloud implementation using virtualization for one of the fortune 500 company.

He also played active role in provisioning infrastructure for one of the largest cash transfer programme in the world.

I would like to thank my wife, Rajnita, and my sons, Henderson and Tiraj, who supported and encouraged me in spite of all the time I took away from them while writing this book.

I also want to thank Nikhil Karkal and Samantha Gonsalves, without whose efforts and encouragement this book quite possibly would not have happened.

I would also like to thank all the reviewers for providing valuable input and making this book a success.

About the Reviewers

Tigran Babloyan is a software developer and technical solution lead with over 8 years of commercial application development and consulting experience. He has played key roles in several Java Enterprise projects for companies such as Sun Microsystems, Oracle, DHL, and several governmental projects. Currently, besides his main duties as a Java development lead, he also consults several companies and start-ups on big data and NoSQL migration. Apache Lucene and Spark, Couchbase, and JavaEE are only a small part of Tigran's daily duties.

Clive Holloway is a New York based developer who has been working with web technologies for over 20 years — from website and mobile UI design, to systems architecture and database design. Surprisingly, he has a website: `http://cliveholloway.net`.

Marcus Johansson is currently working as a Berlin-based freelance developer, having previously worked on one of the world's most visited Couchbase projects during his time at Nokia.

Marcus writes about development in general and Drupal specifically at `www.drupaldare.com`.

www.PacktPub.com

Support files, eBooks, discount offers, and more

For support files and downloads related to your book, please visit www.PacktPub.com.

Did you know that Packt offers eBook versions of every book published, with PDF and ePub files available? You can upgrade to the eBook version at www.PacktPub.com and as a print book customer, you are entitled to a discount on the eBook copy. Get in touch with us at service@packtpub.com for more details.

At www.PacktPub.com, you can also read a collection of free technical articles, sign up for a range of free newsletters and receive exclusive discounts and offers on Packt books and eBooks.

https://www2.packtpub.com/books/subscription/packtlib

Do you need instant solutions to your IT questions? PacktLib is Packt's online digital book library. Here, you can search, access, and read Packt's entire library of books.

Why subscribe?

- Fully searchable across every book published by Packt
- Copy and paste, print, and bookmark content
- On demand and accessible via a web browser

Free access for Packt account holders

If you have an account with Packt at www.PacktPub.com, you can use this to access PacktLib today and view 9 entirely free books. Simply use your login credentials for immediate access.

Table of Contents

Preface

This book will enable you to understand Couchbase, how its flexible schema helps to develop agile application without downtime, and its architecture. You will also learn how to design document base data schema, connecting using connection polling from Java base applications to Couchbase. You will understand how to retrieve data from it using MapReduce based views, understand SQL-like syntax, N1QL to extract documents from the Couchbase database, bucket and perform high availability features with XDCR. It will also enable you to perform full text search by integrating ElasticSearch plugins.

What this book covers

Chapter 1, *Introduction to Couchbase*, introduces the concepts of NoSQL databases, provides the architecture, and introduces the various concepts of Couchbase. It will explain the installation of Couchbase in the Windows and Linux environments; finally, it will introduce the various logging and configuration folders.

Chapter 2, *The Couchbase Administration Interface*, provides an overview on various administration interfaces provided by Couchbase. The reader will be able to use the various interfaces, such as the web admin UI, the administration REST API, and the command line interface.

Chapter 3, *Storing Documents in Couchbase Using Buckets*, introduces the concept of buckets in detail. It will also explain how documents are stored in Couchbase and how it maintains them in a Couchbase cluster.

Chapter 4, *Designing a Document for Couchbase*, introduces the concepts of JSON, compares NoSQL with RDBMS, and explains how to manage relationships between various documents. It will also familiarize you with the document editor option for creating and editing documents using the web UI.

Chapter 5, *Introducing Client SDK*, explains the Couchbase SDK, focusing on the Java API. We will also explore some APIs that are used to connect to Couchbase and perform CRUD operations. It will also explain various concepts, such as locking and counters. The chapter further explains connection management of SDK.

Chapter 6, *Retrieving Documents without Keys Using Views*, explains the concepts of MapReduce, explain the concepts of views and reduce functions. It will also explain filtering and advanced concepts of views, along with retrieving geospatial data.

Chapter 7, *Understanding SQL-Like Queries N1QL*, introduces you to N1QL and explains how to retrieve documents using SQL-like syntax.

Chapter 8, *Full Text Search Using ElasticSearch*, explains how to provide full text search using ElasticSearch plugins. It will explain how to configure ElasticSearch plugins to connect to Couchbase.

Chapter 9, *Data Replication and Compaction*, explains cross datacenter replication for intercluster. It also explains how data compaction happens in the Couchbase cluster.

Chapter 10, *Administration, Tuning, and Monitoring*, explains how to monitor, tune, and configure the Couchbase cluster. Along the way, we will explore some best practices as well. We will also see how to initiate data rebalancing, backing up, and so on.

Chapter 11, *Case Study – An E-Commerce Application*, explains a case on e-commerce and builds it using various features provided by Couchbase, such as document design, views, and so on.

What you need for this book

This book requires Couchbase Enterprise Edition 3.0 to be installed on your machine, so that you can try various features discussed in this book. While writing applications to connect to the Couchbase cluster, you will be using Couchbase Client and Java SDK 2.0, which can be downloaded using Maven 3.0. We will be writing code using Eclipse Lunar IDE. To understand full text search, you need to install the ElasticSearch cluster and plugins to fetch data from Couchbase to ElasticSearch for indexing. Subsequently, you require Apache Tomcat 8.0 to deploy web application.

Who this book is for

If you are new to the NoSQL document system or have little or no experience in NoSQL development and administration and are planning to deploy Couchbase for your next project, then this book is for you. It will be helpful to have a bit of familiarity with Java.

Conventions

In this book, you will find a number of text styles that distinguish between different kinds of information. Here are some examples of these styles and an explanation of their meaning.

Code words in text, database table names, folder names, filenames, file extensions, pathnames, dummy URLs, user input, and Twitter handles are shown as follows: "You can use the rpm command to install Couchbase on Red Hat or CentOS."

A block of code is set as follows:

```
<dependencies>
    <dependency>
        <groupId>com.couchbase.client</groupId>
        <artifactId>java-client</artifactId>
        <version>2.1.3</version>
    </dependency>
</dependencies>
```

Any command-line input or output is written as follows:

```
#/etc/init.d/couchbase-server start
#/etc/init.d/couchbase-server stop
```

New terms and **important words** are shown in bold. Words that you see on the screen, for example, in menus or dialog boxes, appear in the text like this: "Clicking the **Next** button moves you to the next screen."

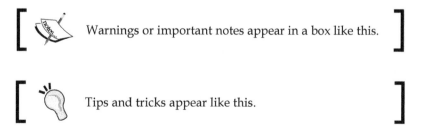

Warnings or important notes appear in a box like this.

Tips and tricks appear like this.

Reader feedback

Feedback from our readers is always welcome. Let us know what you think about this book—what you liked or disliked. Reader feedback is important for us as it helps us develop titles that you will really get the most out of.

To send us general feedback, simply e-mail `feedback@packtpub.com`, and mention the book's title in the subject of your message.

If there is a topic that you have expertise in and you are interested in either writing or contributing to a book, see our author guide at `www.packtpub.com/authors`.

Customer support

Now that you are the proud owner of a Packt book, we have a number of things to help you to get the most from your purchase.

Downloading the example code

You can download the example code files from your account at `http://www.packtpub.com` for all the Packt Publishing books you have purchased. If you purchased this book elsewhere, you can visit `http://www.packtpub.com/support` and register to have the files e-mailed directly to you.

Errata

Although we have taken every care to ensure the accuracy of our content, mistakes do happen. If you find a mistake in one of our books—maybe a mistake in the text or the code—we would be grateful if you could report this to us. By doing so, you can save other readers from frustration and help us improve subsequent versions of this book. If you find any errata, please report them by visiting `http://www.packtpub.com/submit-errata`, selecting your book, clicking on the **Errata Submission Form** link, and entering the details of your errata. Once your errata are verified, your submission will be accepted and the errata will be uploaded to our website or added to any list of existing errata under the Errata section of that title.

To view the previously submitted errata, go to `https://www.packtpub.com/books/content/support` and enter the name of the book in the search field. The required information will appear under the **Errata** section.

Piracy

Piracy of copyrighted material on the Internet is an ongoing problem across all media. At Packt, we take the protection of our copyright and licenses very seriously. If you come across any illegal copies of our works in any form on the Internet, please provide us with the location address or website name immediately so that we can pursue a remedy.

Please contact us at copyright@packtpub.com with a link to the suspected pirated material.

We appreciate your help in protecting our authors and our ability to bring you valuable content.

Questions

If you have a problem with any aspect of this book, you can contact us at questions@packtpub.com, and we will do our best to address the problem.

Introduction to Couchbase

1

This chapter will introduce a new type of database technology called NoSQL. You too are a contributor to the evolution of this technology. Surprised? You do have a Facebook account, upload pictures, and use messenger services, such as WeChat, WhatsApp, right? The data in these are generated at a fast rate and in huge amounts (terabytes per day). They also vary in format or structure. We usually use the term big data for such types of data. Such large amounts of data can't be handled by a traditional relational database management system. That is why a new way needs to be discovered to solve this. This is how NoSQL came into existence. This chapter will introduce you to NoSQL and its fundamentals. Next, you will be introduced to one of the fastest NoSQL databases in the world, called Couchbase. Right, you read it correct! It's the fastest database since all of the data is, by default, cached in the RAM or volatile memory, and the most interesting part is that you don't need to do any configuration for caching the data. Everything will be taken care of by Couchbase Server. Following this, you will learn to install Couchbase Server in Windows and Linux environments. Finally, this chapter will introduce you to the various logs and configuration folders.

In this chapter, we will cover the following topics:

- What is NoSQL and why do we need it?
- Couchbase architecture
- Concepts of Couchbase

What is NoSQL and why do we need it?

It's always a challenge to introduce a new technology, especially when it changes the fundamentals that have been taught for so long. An example is the one I am going to introduce right now. However, it's easy to comprehend it if we understand the rationale behind it. So, let's understand the need for NoSQL. Oh, hold on! We will elaborate on this later.

We are all aware of and use **Relational Database Management Systems** (**RDBMS**). RDBMS is a database management system, which is based on the relational model invented by E. F. Codd, that has features such as normalization, joins, foreign keys, and so on. (Examples of such a database management system would be MySQL, Oracle, DB2 DB, and so on). RDBMS provides features such as transactions, table joins, locking mechanisms, ACID properties, and so on. However, there are some limitations to RDBMS, predominantly in terms of scalability and readiness for schema changes.

> **ACID** stands for Atomicity, Consistency, Isolation, and Durablity. These are properties that are essential for supporting transactions in any database system. In order to guarantee a meaningful and successful transaction, the system has to support all of these properties:
>
> - **Atomicity**: The operation will be performed as a single unit
> - **Consistency**: All the operations will ensure a valid state and consistency of data at the end of the transaction
> - **Isolation**: No two transactions will intervene with each other
> - **Durability**: The transaction will survive system failures

In order to get more clarity, let's look at a scenario. Your organization has recently launched an e-commerce application and you are the technical architect. Everything has been going on smoothly and everyone, including your boss, is happy with the outcome. However, after a couple of months, you start getting complaints from the business team that the application is not performing well. After some investigation, you realize that the consumer base has increased, hence Users traffic has increased. The application server and the infrastructure are not able to handle such an increase in traffic. So what will you do? Think about it. If you are like most other architects, the initial measures would be to scale the application servers, introduce multiple servers, and provide a load balancer, or increase the system resources, such as the RAM and CPU. After you take these steps, the application seems to show some improvement.

But after a couple of weeks comes a realization that the same improvement needs to be done at the database server too. So, what can be done? You have two options:

- Vertical scaling
- Horizontal scaling

The first is vertical scaling, wherein you increase the hardware resources in terms of CPU and RAM. The second is horizontal scaling, wherein you increase the sever nodes.

However, there is a challenge here; we can't just scale the database server horizontally as we do for application servers. If we need to scale database servers horizontally, we need to find a mechanism to distribute data across the servers, balance the load, and what not! The only easy way left is to increase your hardware resources. However, after a certain stage, physical servers can't expand further due to limitations of sockets, chips, and so on, just like if you have four CPU socket servers, then you cannot scale up further than that. Therefore, we need to find a way to scale out, horizontally, when we anticipate an increase in the number of database requests or hits or load in the database layer. Such a situation is encountered in most content-driven, social networking, and e-commerce sites, where there are a large number of transactions taking place in milliseconds.

Besides this, due to dynamics in business functions, the database schema needs to be changed very frequently, which is very common in agile development. It is difficult to incorporate the changes in RDBMS. Sometimes you need to bring the application down to modify the schema, such as adding one column in a table. In order to address such issues, companies such as Facebook and Google started exploring alternatives to RDBMS for data storage that can scale out and handle changes in schemas seamlessly without any impact on business operations. These are the fundamentals of NoSQL.

So what is NoSQL?

NoSQL is a nonrelational database management system that is different from traditional relational database management systems in significant ways. It is designed for distributed data stores in which there are very large-scale data storage requirements (terabytes and petabytes of data). These types of data storage mechanisms may not require fixed schemas, avoid join operations, and typically scale horizontally.

The main feature of NoSQL is that it is schemaless. There is no fixed schema to store data. Also, there is no join between one or more data records or documents. However, nowadays, most of the NoSQL systems have started providing join features. It allows distributed storage and utilizes computing resources, such as CPU and RAM, spanning across the nodes that are part of the NoSQL cluster.

There are different types of NoSQL data stores. Let's try to cover the four main categories of NoSQL systems in brief:

- **Key-value store**: A simple data storage system that uses a key to access values. Some examples are Redis, Riak, and DynamoDB.

  Use Case: Multiplayer online gaming to manage each player session.

- **Column family store**: A sparse matrix system that uses a row and a column as keys, for example, Apache HBase, Apache Cassandra.

  Use Case: Stream massive write loads such as log analysis.

- **Graph store**: This is used for relationship-intensive problems. An example is Neo4j.

  Use Case: Complicated graph problems, such as moving from one point to another.

- **Document store**: This is used to store hierarchical data structures directly in the database, for example, MongoDB (10Gen), CouchDB, and Couchbase.

  Use Case: Storing structured product information.

Why do we need NoSQL?

Electronic data is generated at rapid speed from a variety of sources, such as social media, web server logs, and e-commerce transactions and so on; these include Facebook, Google+, e-commerce websites such as Amazon, eBay, and others. Personal user information, social graphs, geolocation data, user-generated content, and machine logging data are just a few examples of areas in which data has been increasing exponentially. Such data is termed as big data, which usually has a variety of data formats, is generated at a rapid speed, and contains a large set of data. In order to derive information from such big data, large amounts of data have to be processed, for which RDBMS was never designed! The evolution of NoSQL databases is the way to handle such huge data efficiently.

Most of NoSQL databases provide the following benefits:

- It provides a flexible data model. You don't need to worry about the schema. You can design your schema depending on the needs of your application domain and not by storage demands.

- It's scalable and can be done very easily. Since it's a distributed system, it can scale out horizontally without too many changes in the application. In some of the NoSQL systems, such as Couchbase, you can scale out with a few mouse clicks and rebalance it very easily.

- It provides high availability, since there are multiple servers and data are replicated across nodes.

Since NoSQL is a distributed database system, you need to know a theorem called CAP to understand it better, and take better decisions when the system fails in a distributed environment. Let me explain the CAP theorem to you. There are three important properties of this theorem:

- **Consistency**: What comes to your mind when we say *consistency* in a distributed system? When data is replicated to multiple nodes in a distributed system, it should return the same value or state as any of the other replicated nodes. Generally speaking, the data in all nodes must be consistent with each other.

- **Availability**: Systems should be able to serve client requests all the time, irrespective of the situation. In any distributed system, there are multiple nodes and it is ideal that the failure of a node should not stop the availability of the system. In short, the client should be able to perform read, write, and update operations at all times.

- **Partition tolerance**: In any distributed system, depending on an algorithm such as hashing, data or records are partitioned across the nodes or the servers in the database ecosystem. Failures in replicating or transferring data between cluster nodes should not stop the system from responding to client requests. This feature of providing tolerance when there is a disturbance between nodes is called partition tolerance.

The following is a Venn diagram depicting the CAP theorem:

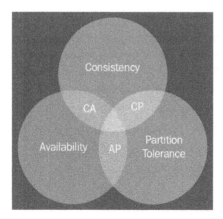

So, you have understood what the CAP properties signify. The CAP theorem states that in any distributed system it can provide only two features out of these three features. Depending on the type of use cases that the system is intended to address, the database system can choose two out of these three features.

There are a number of database systems available in the IT software market—RDBMS such as MySQL, or NoSQL such as MongoDB, Couchbase, Cassandra, and so on. How do you choose a database system that suits your business requirements? This theorem will help you to decide it. In our context, Couchbase has opted for AP—availability and partition tolerance. So, if your application demands availability and partition tolerance more than consistency, you could opt for Couchbase. However, Couchbase provides a feature called eventual consistency, which will be discussed later in *Chapter 6, Retrieving Documents without Keys Using Views*. This feature enables the developer to decide the consistency level per operation.

Having understood what NoSQL is all about and why it's a buzzword nowadays, let's try to understand Couchbase, which is the purpose of this book.

Couchbase Server is a persistent, distributed, document-based database that is part of the NoSQL database movement. It combines the capabilities of Apache CouchDB: document-based and indexing-with that of a Membase database, an integrated RAM caching layer, enabling it to support very fast operations, such as create, store, update, and retrieval.

Couchbase Server is a leading NoSQL database project that focuses on distributed database technology and the surrounding ecosystems. It supports both key-value and document-oriented use cases. All components are available under the Apache 2.0 Public License. It can be obtained as packaged software in both an enterprise edition, which is rigorously tested and provides support, and a community edition that do not have support and is open source.

Let's cover some of the main features of Couchbase Server here:

- **Schemaless**: You don't need to worry about the database schema when changing your application object. Records can have different structures; there is no fixed schema. It allows changes in a data model for rapid application development easily, without the need to perform expensive alter table operations in the database. In short, it provides a flexible data model with JSON support.

- **JSON-based document structure**: The documents in Couchbase are natively stored as JSON. In a document-based NoSQL, metadata of the data like types are stored along with the data and normally all related information is stored together as a single document. When you build an application, you don't require explicit mapping of application objects with that of the database schema. Couchbase provides an interface to create new documents for viewing and editing.

- **Built in clustering with replication**: The Couchbase also provides built-in clustering, wherein all nodes in a cluster are equal. Furthermore, it provides data replication with auto-failover.

- **365 day availability**: The Couchbase cluster provides almost zero downtime maintenance. You can remove a node of the cluster for maintenance and join the cluster after the maintenance operation without suffering any application downtime. High availability of data in the cluster is provided by the replication mechanism.

- **Cache**: By default, all documents are stored in the RAM, and hence provide a built-in managed cache. It provides easy scalability and consistent high performance by adding nodes, thus increasing the RAM in the cluster resources pool.

- **Web UI**: There are simple and easy-to-use admin APIs and UIs provided for smooth administration of the Couchbase cluster. It can also be used to monitor the cluster with ease.

- **Varieties of SDK**: Software development kits for a variety of languages, such as Java, PHP, and so on, are provided to connect to Couchbase Servers.

- In a Couchbase cluster, there are a number of nodes and all nodes are equal; the cluster works on the concept of peer-to-peer. You can easily scale the cluster by adding a node to it. Since all the nodes are the same, there is no single point of failure. The cluster ensures that every node manages some active data and some replica data. The data is distributed across the cluster, and hence the load is also uniformly distributed using auto-sharding. The data is divided into chunks and distributed across the nodes automatically.

 Auto-sharding is a feature of NoSQL databases that spreads documents across the nodes in a cluster automatically. It remains transparent to the application that consumes the data from the cluster.

The architecture of Couchbase

Couchbase clusters consist of multiple nodes. A cluster is a collection of one or more instances of Couchbase server that are configured as a logical cluster. The following is a Couchbase server architecture diagram:

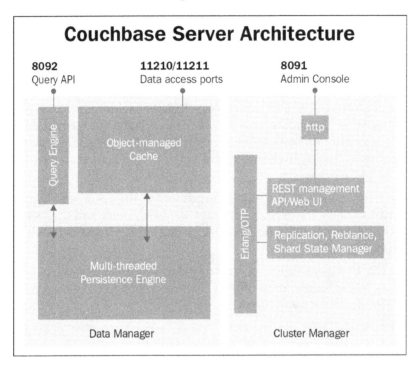

As mentioned earlier, while most of the cluster technologies work on master-slave relationships, Couchbase works on a peer-to-peer node mechanism. This means there is no difference between the nodes in the cluster. The functionality provided by each node is the same. Thus, there is no single point of failure. When there is a failure of one node, another node takes up its responsibility, thus providing high availability.

Data manager

Any operation performed on the Couchbase database system gets stored in the memory, which acts as a caching layer. By default, every document gets stored in the memory for each read, insert, update, and so on, until the memory is full. It's a drop-in replacement for Memcache. However, in order to provide persistency of the record, there is a concept called disk queue. This will flush the record to the disk asynchronously, without impacting the client request. This functionality is provided automatically by the data manager, without any human intervention.

Cluster management

The cluster manager is responsible for node administration and node monitoring within a cluster. Every node within a Couchbase cluster includes the cluster manager component, data storage, and data manager. It manages data storage and retrieval. It contains the memory cache layer, disk persistence mechanism, and query engine.

Couchbase clients use the cluster map provided by the cluster manager to find out which node holds the required data, and then communicate with the data manager on that node to perform database operations.

The Erlang language is used to develop cluster management. Erlang provides a dynamic type system and built-in support for concurrency processes, which are isolated from one another, and are very lightweight in nature. A single Erlang VM, can run a quarter of a million processes. It also provides a lot of modules that help with distributed processing. Moreover, it provides enhancement of debugging and patching live systems is easy compared to any other language.

Concepts of Couchbase

Let's take a look at some of the concepts of Couchbase next in this section.

Buckets

In RDBMS, we usually encapsulate all relevant data for a particular application in a database namespace. Say, for example, we are developing an e-commerce application. We usually create a database name, e-commerce, which will be used as the logical namespace to store records in a table, such as customer or shopping cart details. It's called a bucket in a Couchbase terminology. So, whenever you want to store any document in a Couchbase cluster, you will be creating a bucket as a logical namespace as a first step. A bucket is an independent virtual container that groups documents logically in a Couchbase cluster, which is equivalent to a database namespace in RDBMS. It can be accessed by various clients in an application. You can also configure features such as security, replication, and so on per bucket. We usually create one database and consolidate all related tables in that namespace in the RDBMS development. Likewise, in Couchbase too, you will usually create one bucket per application and encapsulate all the documents in it.

Views

Views enable indexing and querying by looking inside JSON documents for a key, for ranges of keys, or to aggregate data.

Views are created using incremental MapReduce, which powers indexing. We will discuss this in detail in *Chapter 6, Retrieving Documents without Keys Using Views*. You can build complex views for your data using the map reduce feature. Views enable us to define materialized views on JSON documents and then query across the dataset.

 A materialized view is a database object that contains the result of MapReduce.

Using views, you can define primary, simple secondary (the most common use case), complex secondary, tertiary, and composite indexes, as well as aggregations (reduction). It is developed using MapReduce technology. MapReduce functions are written in JavaScript. You will understand more about MapReduce and views in detail in *Chapter 6, Retrieving Documents without Keys Using Views*.

Cross Data Center Replication

Cross Data Center Replication (**XDCR**) is the mechanism provided by Couchbase to replicate documents from one cluster to another. Most of the time, data will be replicated across clusters that are geographically spread out. Usually, when you want to replicate data in a separate data center for disaster recovery or to provide performance by enabling data locality for application, we configure XDCR on a per bucket (per database) basis. When you configure replication across two clusters—say Cluster A is located in Imphal (India) and Cluster B is in Mumbai (India), which are 2,500 kms away from each other—you can specify to replicate only from Cluster A to Cluster B, unidirectional or in both directions, that is, bidirectional. Thus, you are enabling clients to read/write from both the clusters when you enable bidirectional active replication across the clusters. Lastly, you need to remember that this is different from intracluster replication, which occurs within a cluster.

 In case of intracluster replication, documents are replicated as a replica for a failover in the other nodes of the same cluster. More details about XDCR will be discussed in *Chapter 9, Data Replication and Compaction*.

Installation on Windows and Linux environments

Enough of concepts! Let's install Couchbase so that we can get some hands-on experience. We will install in a Windows environment first. You can download the software from www.couchbase.com.

You can download the enterprise or community edition. We will use the Couchbase 64-bit enterprise edition.

To start the installation wizard, double-click on **couchbase-server-enterprise_ x86_64_3.0.0.setup.exe**. Then, you will see the following window:

Click on **Next**. The next screen will allow you to select the folder where you want to install Couchbase. In my case, I chose the default location. You can change the directory location if you want; click on the **Browse** button for that, as shown here:

After selecting the installation folder, you can click on **Install**, as shown in the following screenshot:

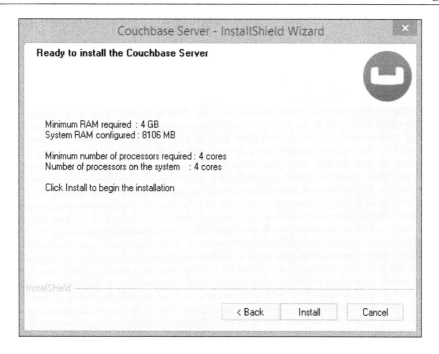

After this, the Couchbase will be installed on your system. You can see the progress of installation in the following screenshot:

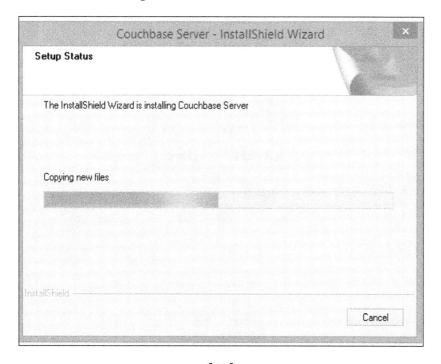

It will take some time to install. After a few minutes, you will see the following success screen. Congratulations!!

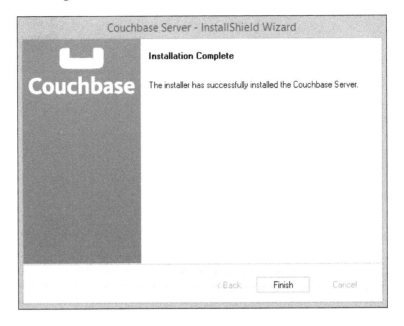

You need to change some settings before you can use Couchbase. You can access the admin console with `http://localhost:8091/index.html`. The default port is `8091`. You can change this if required.

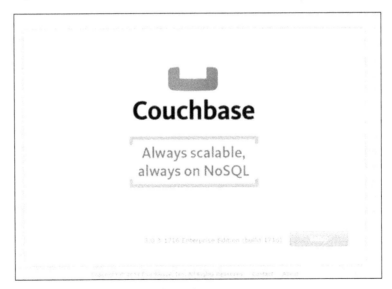

The Bucket set up

Click on **Setup** and you will be able to configure Couchbase for your environment:

Configure Disk Storage

Databases Path: /opt/couchbase/var/lib/couchbase/data

Free: 2 GB

Indices Path: /opt/couchbase/var/lib/couchbase/data

Free: 2 GB

If you use this server in a production, use different file systems for databases and indices.

Join Cluster / Start new Cluster

If you want to add this server to an existing Couchbase Cluster, select "Join a cluster now". Alternatively, you may create a new Couchbase Cluster by selecting "Start a new cluster".

If you start a new cluster the "Per Server RAM Quota" you set below will define the amount of RAM each server provides to the Couchbase Cluster. This value will be inherited by all servers subsequently joining the cluster, so please set appropriately.

⊙ Start a new cluster.

RAM Available: 2026 MB

Per Server RAM Quota: 801   MB (256 MB — 1621 MB)

○ Join a cluster now.

Server configuration

You can select the location of the databases and indexes with this option. Select the options shown in the preceding screenshot. Since it's the first node we are installing and there is no existing cluster, select **Start a new cluster** and specify 801 MB RAM, which needs to be allocated to the Couchbase cluster by each node. Then, click on **Next**:

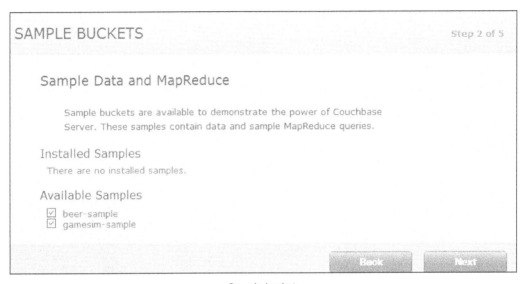

Sample bucket

Select both the samples provided along with the Couchbase software. After that, click on **Next**. On the subsequent page, create a default bucket with the following options:

- RAM: 601 MB
- Replicas: 1

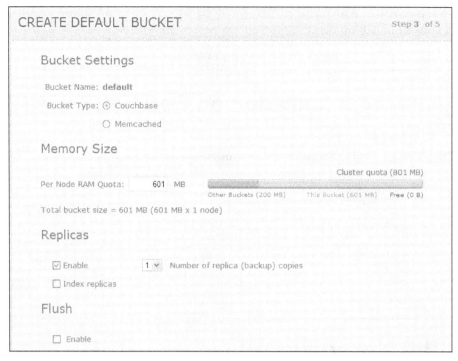

Default bucket

We will explain all these options of bucket settings when we discuss buckets in *Chapter 3, Storing Documents in Couchbase Using Buckets*. Keep clicking on the **Next** button until you get the following screen:

Admin credentials

Enter the password, which is `root123`. It will be used to connect to the Couchbase admin console. Click on **Next** to finish.

Your Couchbase Server is now running and ready to use!

Couchbase installation on Red Hat, CentOS, and others

You can use the `rpm` command to install Couchbase on Red Hat or CentOS, as follows. Replace the version with the version number of the package downloaded:

```
# rpm -ivhcouchbase-server-{version}.rpm
```

For Ubuntu and Debian, use the following:

```
#dpkg -i couchbase-server{version007D.deb
```

After the installation is complete, Couchbase starts automatically. You can perform the initial setup by going to `http://localhost:8091`.

Startup and shutdown

Couchbase gives you the ability to start up and shut down your cluster. Let's take a look at how to achieve this on Linux and Windows.

On Linux

Downloading the example code

You can download the example code files for all Packt books you have purchased from your account at `http://www.packtpub.com`. If you purchased this book elsewhere, you can visit `http://www.packtpub.com/support` and register to have the files e-mailed directly to you.

You can start and stop a Couchbase cluster using the following commands:

```
#/etc/init.d/couchbase-server start
```

```
#/etc/init.d/couchbase-server stop
```

It assumes that you are executing the preceding commands with the root credentials. For some OS you need to use the `sudo` command.

On Windows

You can start and stop a cluster using the scripts provided in the following installation folders:

- `C:\Program Files\Couchbase\Server\bin\service_start.bat`
- `C:\Program Files\Couchbase\Server\bin\service_stop.bat`

Understanding log and configuration files

Couchbase Server creates a number of different log files, depending on the component of the system that produced the error, the level and severity of the problem being reported. All these logs are created in a folder. Whenever there is any issue, you can go to the following paths and check the respective logs. Their specific paths are:

- In Windows:

  `C:\Program Files\Couchbase\Server\var\lib\couchbase\logs`

- In Linux:

  `/opt/couchbase/var/lib/couchbase/logs`

Some of the logs that need to be looked into when there is an issue are discussed next.

debug

You can find debug-level error messages related to the core server management subsystem. This log does not contain information included in the `couchdb`, `xdcr`, and `stats` logs.

info

You can observe information-level error messages related to the core server management subsystem. This log does not contain information included in the `couchdb`, `xdcr`, and `stats` logs.

error

Any error-level messages for all subsystems of Couchbase excluding `xdcr` related errors, will be logged in this file.

mapreduce_errors

Errors pertaining to JavaScript and other view-processing errors are reported in the `mapreduce_errors` file.

reports.log

It logs only the progress report and crash reports for the Erlang process (the language in which the cluster management is being developed), which is a lightweight process that provides built-in support for concurrency, an important requirement for distributed systems.

Mobile development with Couchbase Lite

Couchbase Lite is an embedded JSON database that can work as a standalone server, in a P2P network, or as a remote endpoint for Couchbase Server. It provides native APIs for the iOS and Android platforms. It supports replication with compatible database servers. It also supports low-latency and offline access to data.

The sync server enables Couchbase Server 2.0 and later to act as a replication endpoint for Couchbase Lite. The Sync Gateway runs an HTTP listener process that provides a passive replication endpoint and uses a Couchbase Server bucket as persistent storage for all database documents.

> **Downloading the example code**
>
> You can download the example code files for all Packt books you have purchased from your account at `http://www.packtpub.com`. If you purchased this book elsewhere, you can visit `http://www.packtpub.com/support` and register to have the files e-mailed directly to you.

Summary

This chapter introduced the concepts of NoSQL databases and various features of the Couchbase cluster. It also explained the installation process for Couchbase on Windows and Linux environments. I hope that by now you have some understanding of Couchbase, what it provides, and some of its features.

The next chapter will take you through an overview of Couchbase's administrative interface.

2
The Couchbase
Administration Interface

This chapter will provide an overview of various administration interfaces provided by Couchbase. We will explore the web admin user interface in detail and get an overview of the REST API and CLI. You will be using the web UI extensively to manage the Couchbase cluster with ease. It's one of the easiest and most powerful tools provided by Couchbase for managing its clusters.

In any enterprise software, we require some mechanism to interact with, configure, and monitor. Couchbase provides three main tools for administrating its clusters. They are as follows:

- Web admin UI
- Administration using the REST API
- Command line interface

Let's explore each of these options one by one. Before we start exploring each of these tools, we will cover some concepts that you are required to understand to perform various administrative tasks in the cluster.

The need for the Couchbase administrative interface

Couchbase has been designed to make the life of an administrator easy. As seen in the previous chapter, it can be installed with a few clicks, and most of the administrative tasks that are required for running and configuring clusters are managed by the Couchbase server itself. In fact, Couchbase provides very minimal configuration options to bring the cluster up and running, and the majority of these configurations can be performed through a very user-friendly user interface. In most cases, the administrator does not have to make any changes in configuration, unless required.

However, in any system, some operational tasks and maintenance are required to be performed for smooth operation and to keep the system healthy. For instance, when the load on the cluster increases, we can expand it by adding nodes to increase the memory and improve the disk I/O performance. Couchbase provides a mechanism to expand the cluster size when the application load increases, and also to trim the cluster size down during a lean period, instantly without any complication. If there is a need to increase the memory, then with a few clicks, the administrator can add servers to the cluster, and remove them easily whenever there is no load on the cluster. Sometimes, a particular node in the cluster holds more data than that of average nodes in the cluster, then it needs to distribute the data across the cluster evenly to balance load, which in turns improve performance. This process is called **rebalancing**. The rebalancing process can be performed online, while the cluster is serving the regular data requests.

Although buckets can be created from the client **Software Development Kit** (**SDK**) using various APIs, sometimes the administrator needs to create them and view the documents stored in the bucket manually. Moreover, administrators need to monitor the health of the Couchbase cluster and take measures depending on various parameters to provide optimal performance. Since, a Couchbase cluster usually consists of multiple nodes, there is a high chance of intermittent node failure. When a node in a cluster fails for different reasons, such as when hardware or software corruption occurred, the administrator should be able to determine the failed node and the reason for it's failure. Although Couchbase is designed to manage itself, such as automated failover of nodes, the cluster can be configured to control failure manually. When a cluster node fails, Couchbase ensures that passive replicas are moved to active replicas for those documents that were active in the failed nodes in the other data nodes of the cluster.

Clusters can have issues such as performance, low disk space when there is high fragmentation of a bucket, and so on. Monitoring such issues and fine-tuning to resolve them can be done through the admin UI.

Moreover, administrators need to perform regular backups to prevent data loss or for disaster recovery. Although Couchbase replicates data across the nodes within a cluster, it is a good practice to take a backup of data on a regular basis for statuary compliance and recovery when disasters strike. Such tasks and maintenance can be performed using the aforementioned tools.

The web admin UI

Now, let's understand and explore the main administrative web user interface provided for managing Couchbase clusters. It provides a complete interface for configuring, managing, and monitoring Couchbase clusters.

Some of the main functionalities it provides are as follows:

- The administrator can view the overall health of the Couchbase cluster
- The administrator can create data buckets, perform configuration, and modify various properties related to buckets
- The administrator can view active nodes, their configuration, and perform overall operations in the cluster

The web UI provides various tabs that can be used to view cluster information, details of the server nodes, information about data buckets, view configuration, the configuration options for XDCR (for data replication), logging and setting of the cluster name, and so on.

The web admin UI - the settings tab

The **Cluster Overview** section provides an overview of the Couchbase cluster status. It's the home page of the web console. The administrator can take a glance at the overall status of the cluster from a single window:

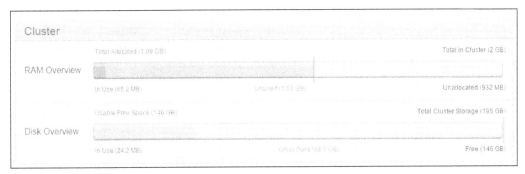

The web console - A cluster overview

The **Cluster** section provides information about the RAM and disk usage for the cluster. As shown in the preceding screenshot, out of an overall cluster with a total memory size of 2 GB RAM, approximately 1.09 GB is allocated to the default bucket. The total memory/cache size of the cluster is 2 GB, since we have configured a 2 GB RAM quota for each server contributing to the cluster at the time of installation. Currently, we have only one node in our cluster.

The total cluster disk size is the total space of the drive in which the Couchbase node is being installed. In our case, we have installed it in the `c:` drive and its capacity is 195 GB. Out of this, 146 GB is free, as shown here:

Drive capacity usage

Buckets and servers

You already have an idea about buckets from the first chapter. You can view its features from the web console as shown in the following screenshot:

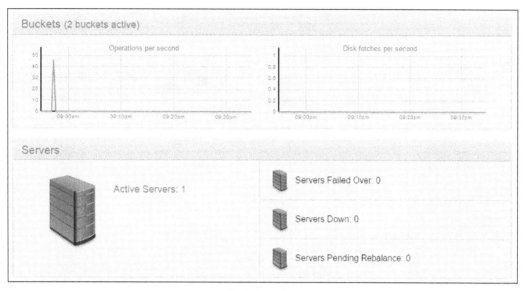

Bucket overview

The **Buckets** section allows administrators to observe read/write operations per second and disk I/O of the top active buckets. The administrator can determine the operation load on buckets from this section.

The **Servers** section provides some hints on how many nodes there are in the cluster, how many servers have a failed status, and whether there are any servers that require rebalancing after joining the cluster.

The **Data Buckets** view provides two graphs showing the operations per second and disk fetches per second.

Server nodes

When you click on the **Server Nodes** tab, you will be shown the system resources usage by all nodes that are part of the cluster. You can expand an individual node and view its details.

System resources by node

You will find a warning that displays on the screen stating that the cluster requires at least two nodes when you configure replication on a bucket. This is obvious since at least two nodes are required in a cluster for replication, one for the active and another for the passive replica.

In this section, the administrator can find the nodes that require rebalancing of data.

Data buckets

The **Data Buckets** section provides views on data buckets created in the cluster. The administrator can also create buckets and modify its settings using this option.

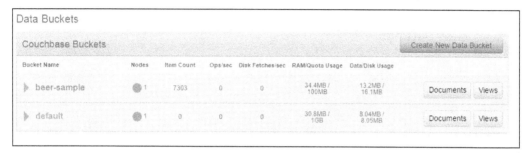

The Data Bucket view

You can determine the settings of a bucket by expanding it. Let's expand the **beer-sample** bucket to view its details.

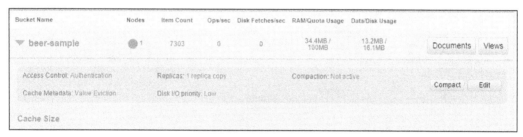

Bucket setting info

You can now view comprehensive details about the bucket. You can also verify whether access to the bucket requires authentication or not. What's more, you can determine the replication factor and configure it for the bucket using this console. You can even perform compaction and defragmentation of disks from this console using the **Compact** button. More on compaction in *Chapter 9, Data Replication and Compaction*.

And finally, you can edit the bucket's settings using the **Edit** button, as displayed in the following screenshot:

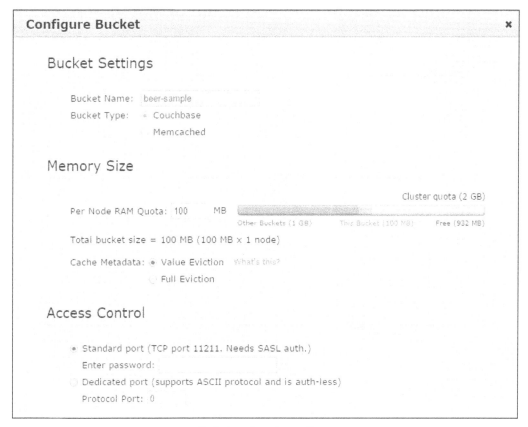

Bucket configuration options

Click on the **Documents** button to view documents in the bucket. You can edit and delete a document using this console. You can even search a particular document using the **Document ID**, which will be explained later.

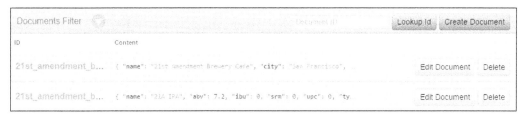

The document editor

Most of the time, administrators need to create buckets for each application. This can be done using the **Create New Data Bucket** button on the **Data Buckets** tab. Let's now create a new data bucket, as follows:

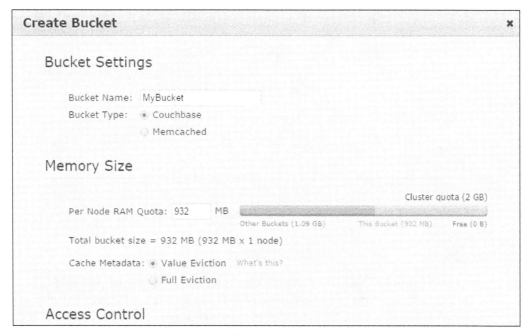

Bucket creation

Under the **Create Bucket** window, the administrator needs to add a few details to create a new bucket, as explained in the following:

- **Bucket Settings**: Here, the administrator can enter the name of the bucket; let's use MyBucket, in our case. Out of the two options, you can select the type of bucket as **Couchbase** for the time being.

> The following are the types of bucket:
>
> **Memcached**: This stores documents in the memory only, hence volatile in nature.
>
> **Couchbase**: This gives persistence to documents by flushing documents on disks.
>
> Further details will be provided in the next chapter.

- **Memory Size**: Specify the RAM size that needs to be allocated from each node of the cluster for this bucket.

Access Control

- Standard port (TCP port 11211. Needs SASL auth.)

  Enter password: ••••••••

- Dedicated port (supports ASCII protocol and is auth-less)

  Protocol Port:

Replicas

- ☑ Enable   1 ▾ Number of replica (backup) copies

- ☐ Index replicas   Warning: you do not have enough servers to support this number of replicas.

Bucket creation continued

- **Access Control**: There are two options under this — **Standard port** and **Dedicated port**. You can choose **Standard port** and enter the password as Mybucket to secure the bucket when connecting to it from clients.

> The user ID used to connect to the bucket will be the name of the bucket itself. If you want to make changes to the port number to connect to the bucket using the SDK, you can choose the **Dedicated port** option and enter the desired port number. Note that the **Dedicated port** option will not require authentication, and hence, no password!

- **Replicas**: If there is a need to store the same document on different nodes, replicas need to be enabled. This can be done by selecting the **Enable** checkbox.

> The administrator can configure up to three replicas per bucket. You will get a warning when you have fewer nodes than required for a configured replica. You can also configure the bucket to replicate indexes by selecting the **Index replicas** checkbox.

Disk I/O Optimization

Set the bucket disk I/O priority: ◉ Low (default)   What's this?
                                    ○ High

Auto-Compaction

Auto-Compaction settings trigger the compaction process. The process comparts databases and their respective view indexes when the following conditions are met.

☐ Override the default autocompaction settings?

Flush

☐ Enable   What's this?

                                                              Cancel   Create

Bucket creation continued

- **Disk I/O Optimization**: The administrator can set this option to either **Low**, which is the default option, or **High**.

- **Auto-Compaction**: By checking this option, you instruct Couchbase to automatically rebuild the stored data and its indexes in order to reduce fragmentation of data.

- **Flush**: The administrator can enable this to run the Flush command, which deletes all documents inside a bucket.

 Ideally, you should not enable Flush in a production environment so as to avoid accidental flushing. You can enable this option when a temporary bucket is created for an ad hoc requirement.

Click on **Create**. Now, you can view **MyBucket** on the console, as shown here:

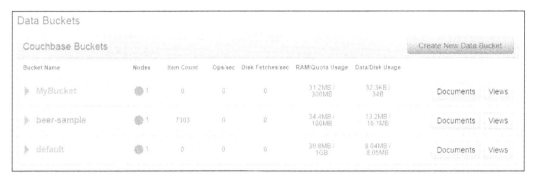

Bucket overview

Views

Administrators can create and manage the **Views** function for indexing and querying data using the **Views** tab. You can preview the results from views using this tab. More details about views will be discussed in *Chapter 6, Retrieving Documents without Keys Using Views.*

XDCR

The **XDCR** section is used to create and configure cross data center replication, which will be explained in detail in *Chapter 9, Data Replication and Compaction.*

Log

Errors and problems can be viewed from the **Log** tab, as shown in the following screenshot:

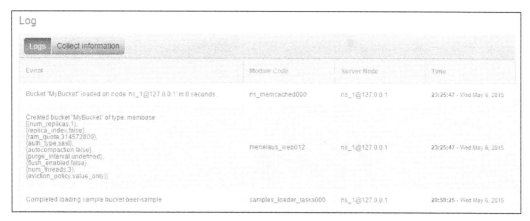

Log view

Whenever there is any critical issue and a call needs to be logged with Couchbase, you can upload logs from the cluster or individual nodes using the **Collect** button, as shown in the following screenshot:

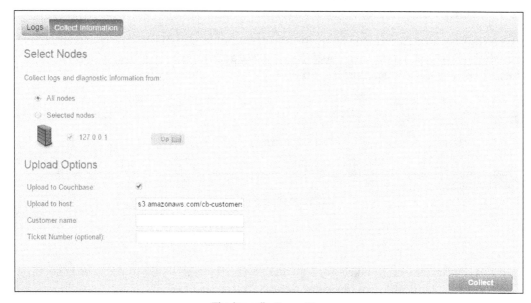

The log collection setting

Settings

The administrator can assign a cluster name using the **Settings** option of the **Cluster** tab. You can assign the RAM size that will contribute to the Couchbase cluster by each node in this section.

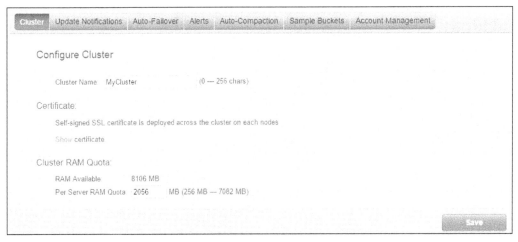

Cluster name settings

You can use the **Update Notifications** feature, if you want to be notified when a new version of Couchbase server is available.

The administrator can enable an auto-failover when a node fails after a certain threshold timeout. To do this, check the **Enable auto-failover** option under the **Auto-Failover** tab and specify the timeout period, as shown here:

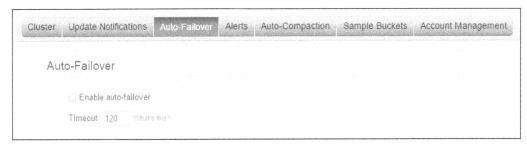

Auto-Failover settings

You can configure e-mail alerts for various alerts, that are listed in the **Alerts** section. You need to specify the e-mail server details in this section.

Auto-Compaction provides options to configure settings related to compaction, which we will explore in more detail in *Chapter 9, Data Replication and Compaction*. For the time being, you can skip this.

If you forgot to load the sample buckets while configuring, after installation, it can be done using **Sample Buckets**.

Account Management provides options to create a read-only user for the cluster. This can be used when you require an administrator with read-only rights.

That's it from the web UI perspective.

Couchbase administrative REST API

Another way to administrate Couchbase clusters is by using the REST API. It provides all the features we have discussed in the web console. In fact, the REST API is being used behind the scenes for most of the options displayed in the web console. You can perform all administrative functionalities using the REST API too.

You need some REST API tools to use this feature. In our case, we will use curl. It can be downloaded and installed from http://curl.haxx.se/download.html.

We will see an example as follows. You can refer the Couchbase documentation for comprehensive details on the REST API usages and syntax:

```
curl -u Administrator:root123 http://localhost:8091/pools/default
```

This command provides cluster details in a JSON document.

The REST API output

You can get information about a specific bucket that is `LearningCouchbase` using the following command:

```
curl -u Administrator:root123
http://localhost:8091/pools/default/buckets/LearningCouchbase
```

You need to pass the user ID and password credentials to connect to the cluster using the `-u` parameter.

The command line interface

Couchbase also provides the CLI to interact with the Couchbase cluster. You can perform almost all the functionalities that were performed using the web console by using CLI. Since most administrative activities can be performed using the web UI, it won't be explained here due to space constraints. Let me provide a sample command for better understanding. However, you can refer to the Couchbase documentation for details.

You can find all CLI tools in the installation folder. In our case, the installation folder is at `C:\Program Files\Couchbase\Server\bin`. For Linux, you can find this at `/opt/couchbase/bin` path.

In order to determine all the buckets in a cluster, you can execute the following command:

```
couchbase-cli bucket-list -c localhost:8091 -u Administrator -p
root123
```

This is what the output looks like:

```
C:\Program Files\Couchbase\Server\bin>couchbase-cli bucket-list -c localhost:809
1 -u Administrator -p root123
MyBucket
 bucketType: membase
 authType: sasl
 saslPassword: mybucket
 numReplicas: 1
 ramQuota: 314572800
 ramUsed: 32128360
beer-sample
 bucketType: membase
 authType: sasl
 saslPassword:
 numReplicas: 1
 ramQuota: 104857600
 ramUsed: 36136904
default
 bucketType: membase
 authType: sasl
 saslPassword:
 numReplicas: 1
 ramQuota: 1073741824
 ramUsed: 32312656
```

The `couchbase-cli` command accepts the `bucket-list` parameters to view all buckets in the cluster which is specified with the `-c` parameter.

Summary

This chapter introduced various features provided by the web UI for configuring and monitoring the Couchbase cluster. You have learned how to create bucket and configure node settings in the cluster. Then, we explored how to manage the Couchbase cluster using the REST API and CLI options.

In the next chapter, we will explore documents and understand what documents are all about. We will also discuss JSON and its representation of documents in a Couchbase cluster. We will also explore more about buckets and its configurations.

3
Storing Documents in Couchbase Using Buckets

This chapter introduces the concept of buckets in detail. It will explain how documents are stored in Couchbase and how they are maintained in a Couchbase cluster. We will explore the various types of bucket and their usage. You will also understand in detail the various parts of documents that are stored in a bucket. Besides buckets and documents, you will also understand the internal mechanisms of Couchbase, including ejection, replication, warmup, rebalancing, and so on.

Buckets

We already came across the term bucket in the previous chapter. Now, let me explain this concept in detail, since it's the component that administrators and developers will be working with most of the time. In fact, I used to wonder why it is named "bucket". Perhaps, we can store anything in it as we do in the physical world, hence the name "bucket". In any database system, the main purpose is to store data, and the logical namespace for storing data is called a database. Likewise, in Couchbase, the namespace for storing data is called a bucket. So in brief, it's a data container that stores data related to applications, either in RAM or in disks.

In fact, buckets help you to partition application data depending on an application's requirements. If you are hosting different types of applications in a cluster, say an e-commerce application and a data warehouse, you can partition them using buckets. You can create two buckets, one for the e-commerce application and another for the data warehouse. As a thumb rule, you create one bucket for each application. In an RDBMS, we store data in the form of rows in a table, which in turn is encapsulated by a database.

In Couchbase, a bucket is the equivalence of a database, but there is no concept of tables in Couchbase. In Couchbase, all data or records, which are referred to as documents, are stored directly in a bucket. Basically, the lowest namespace for storing documents or data in Couchabase is a bucket.

Internally, Couchbase stores documents in different storages for different buckets. Information such as runtime statistics is collected and reported by the Couchbase cluster, grouped by the bucket type. It enables you to flush out the documents from individual buckets. You can create a separate temporary bucket rather than a regular transaction bucket when you need temporary storage for ad hoc requirements, such as reporting, temporary workspace for application programming, and so on, so that you can flush out the temporary bucket after use. The features or capabilities of a bucket depend on its type, which will be discussed subsequently.

Types of bucket

Couchbase provides two types of bucket differentiated by the mechanism of their storage and capabilities. The two types are:

- Memcached
- Couchbase

Memcached

As the name suggests, buckets of the Memcached type store documents in the memory, RAM only. This means that documents stored in the Memcache bucket are volatile in nature. Hence, such types of buckets won't survive a system reboot or failures. Documents that are stored in such buckets will be accessible by direct address using the key-value pair mechanism. The bucket is distributed, which means that it is spread across the Couchbase cluster nodes. Since it's volatile in nature, you need to be sure of its use cases before using such types of buckets. You can use this kind of bucket to store data; that is required temporarily and for better performance, since all of the data is stored in the memory but doesn't require durability. Suppose you need to display a list of countries in your application, then, instead of always fetching data from the disk storage, the best way is to fetch data from the disk, populate it in the Memcached bucket, and use it in your application. In the Memcached bucket, the maximum size of a document allowed is 1 MB. All of the data is stored in RAM, and if the bucket is running out of memory, the oldest data will be discarded. We can't replicate a Memcached bucket. It's completely compatible with the open source Memcached distributed memory object caching system. If you want to know more about the Memcached technology, you can refer to `http://memcached.org/`.

Couchbase

The Couchbase bucket type gives persistence to documents. It is distributed across a cluster of nodes and can configure replication, which is not supported in the Memcached bucket type. It's highly available, since documents are replicated across nodes in a cluster.

Let's try to understand some of the capabilities provided by the Couchbase bucket so that we can design or configure buckets efficiently. Initially, whenever data is inserted in a bucket by a client, it gets stored in the memory, and is subsequently pushed to the disk storage using different queue processes. Hence, all documents are persisted to the disk subsequently to survive system reboots, crashes, and so on. Currently, you can configure a maximum of three replicas per bucket. This type of bucket enables load balancing across the entire cluster by providing dynamic addition and removal of nodes to the cluster.

 The maximum document size allowed by a Couchbase bucket is 20 MB. The main advantage of the Couchbase bucket over the Memcached bucket is that data stored in the Couchbase bucket survives system crashes, since it is stored in the disk. Moreover, you can perform cluster activities online while user services are being provided uninterrupted.

So, how do we create a bucket? Hope you still remember! We explored this in *Chapter 2, The Couchbase Administration Interface*. You can refer to this if you can't recall it. Bucket-related information can be viewed using the web console, as follows:

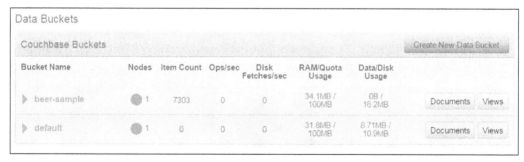

Bucket Name	Nodes	Item Count	Ops/sec	Disk Fetches/sec	RAM/Quota Usage	Data/Disk Usage		
▶ beer-sample	● 1	7303	0	0	34.1MB / 100MB	0B / 16.2MB	Documents	Views
▶ default	● 1	0	0	0	31.8MB / 100MB	8.71MB / 10.9MB	Documents	Views

The bucket view

Let me show you another way of creating a bucket using CLI if you are the kind of administrator who is comfortable with commands:

```
couchbase-cli bucket-create -c 192.168.0.1:8091 -u Administrator -p
root123
        --bucket=LearningCouchbase
        --bucket-type=couchbase
        --bucket-port=11222
        --bucket-ramsize=100
        --bucket-replica=1
```

You need to open a command window. Then go to the `bin` folder, which is inside the Couchbase installation folder and execute the preceding command.

```
D:\Couchbase\bin>
D:\Couchbase\bin>
D:\Couchbase\bin>couchbase-cli bucket-create -c localhost:8091 -u Administrator
-p root123  --bucket=LearningCouchbase  --bucket-type=couchbase  --bucket-port=1
1222  --bucket-ramsize=100  --bucket-replica=1
SUCCESS: bucket-create

D:\Couchbase\bin>
```

The Couchbase CLI

We can view the bucket details in the web console after the preceding command is executed successfully. The **LearningCouchbase** bucket is shown in the following screenshot:

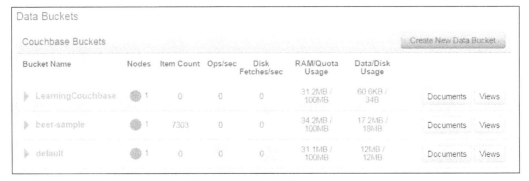

Bucket Name	Nodes	Item Count	Ops/sec	Disk Fetches/sec	RAM/Quota Usage	Data/Disk Usage		
▶ LearningCouchbase	1	0	0	0	31.2MB / 100MB	60.6KB / 34B	Documents	Views
▶ beer-sample	1	7303	0	0	34.2MB / 100MB	17.2MB / 18MB	Documents	Views
▶ default	1	0	0	0	31.1MB / 100MB	12MB / 12MB	Documents	Views

The Couchbase UI - Bucket Console

Most of the time, we need to modify the various options of a bucket after it is created, to improve performance or for business requirements. These can be performed using the CLI or the web console. Let's explore some common options that are provided by the web UI to modify buckets. You are allowed to modify each of the node's RAM quota, the access control port, enable flushing of the bucket, and so on.

> You are not allowed to change the bucket type once it is created; hence, ensure that you choose the right bucket type while creating a bucket.

Whenever you need to modify a bucket, you can click on the **Edit** button, which can be found after clicking on the desired bucket in the bucket console and expanding the vertical arrows against the left of the bucket name. You will see a user interface as shown in the following screenshot. You can even delete the bucket from this UI.

Configure Bucket   ✕

Bucket Settings

Bucket
Name: LearningCouchbase

Bucket Type: ● Couchbase
              ○ Memcached

Memory Size

Cluster quota (1 GB)

Per Node RAM Quota: 100
MB   Other Buckets   This Bucket (100   Free (724
Total bucket size = 100 MB (100(200 MB)   MB)   MB)
MB x 1 node)

Cache Metadata: ● Value Eviction   What's this?
                 ○ Full Eviction

Access Control

○ Standard port (TCP port 11211. Needs SASL auth.)
Enter password:
● Dedicated port (supports ASCII protocol and is auth-less)
Protocol Port: 11222

Bucket settings

An administrator can even initiate compaction on a bucket using the **Compact** button, which is on the left of the **Edit** button in the bucket console, and the progress of the compaction process can be seen at the top-right corner of the screen, as shown in the following screenshot:

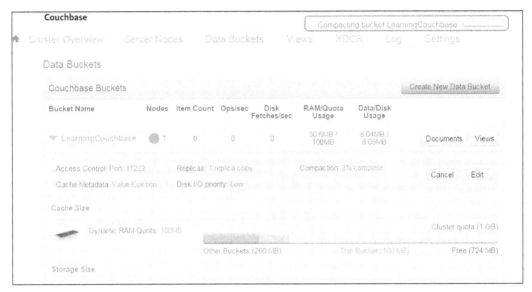

Bucket information

If you have observed, the data bucket's console properly, you might noticed a bucket named **default**. This is a default bucket provided by Couchbase that runs on the default port no. `11211` without authentication. It is automatically set up at the time of installation. You can remove it if it is not required.

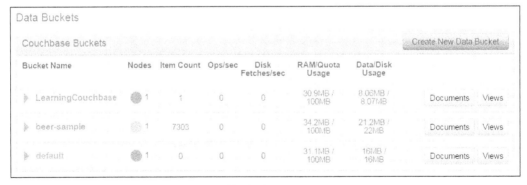

The bucket view

Before we move ahead to understand documents in detail, let's understand how a bucket stores documents, retrieves it, and ensures performance to a client. We always say that Couchbase provides high performance for data storage and retrieval. This is possible due to an inbuilt caching layer that comprises RAM from all nodes that are part of the Couchbase cluster. Bucket data consists of documents that are stored in RAM along with the documents that are spilled on disks. This entire mechanism of storing documents in the memory and spilling them over to the disk is taken care of automatically by the Couchbase cluster. Couchbase maintains a working set of data in the RAM that is often accessed by its client application. It's worth understanding a mechanism call's eventual persistence, which writes data from the memory to the disk while client access is being served from the RAM itself by the cluster during the process. This process enables Couchbase to provide high read performance by serving requests from the RAM itself, all the time.

Understanding documents

By now, you must have understood the concept of buckets, its working and configuration, and so on. Let's now understand the items that get stored in buckets. So, what is a document? A document is a piece of information or data that gets stored in a bucket. It's the smallest item that can be stored in a bucket. As a developer, you will always be working on a bucket, in terms of documents. Documents are similar to a row in the RDBMS table schema but, in NoSQL terminologies, it will be referred to as a document. It's a way of thinking and designing data objects. All information and data should get stored as a document as if it were a physical document. All NoSQL databases, including Couchbase, don't require a fixed schema to store documents or data in a particular bucket. These documents are represented in the form of JSON. Further information and design practices for a document, along with JSON, will be discussed in the next chapter. For the time being, let's try to understand documents at a basic level.

Let me show you how a document is represented in Couchbase for better clarity. You need to install the **beer-sample** bucket for this, which comes along with the Couchbase software installation. If you did not install it earlier, you can do it from the web console using the **Settings** button.

```
beer-sample                  ▾  > Documents

21st_amendment_brewery_cafe                            Delete   Save As   Save

 1  {
 2      "name": "21st Amendment Brewery Cafe",
 3      "city": "San Francisco",
 4      "state": "California",
 5      "code": "94107",
 6      "country": "United States",
 7      "phone": "1-415-369-0900",
 8      "website": "http://www.21st-amendment.com/",
 9      "type": "brewery",
10      "updated": "2010-10-24 13:54:07",
11      "description": "The 21st Amendment Brewery offers a variety of award winning house made brews and American
12      "address": [
13          "563 Second Street"
14      ],
15      "geo": {
16          "accuracy": "ROOFTOP",
17          "lat": 37.7825,
18          "lon": -122.393
19      }
20  }
```

Document overview

The preceding screenshot shows a document, it represents a brewery and its document ID is **21st_amendment_brewery_cafe**. Each document can have multiple properties/items along with its values. For example, **name** is the property and **21st Amendment Brewery Café** is the value of the name property.

So, what is this document ID? The document ID is a unique identifier that is assigned for each document in a bucket. You need to assign a unique ID whenever a document gets stored in a bucket. It's just like the primary key of a table in RDBMS.

A document can be nested, that is, it can have another document inside it. In our preceding example, **geo** is a property that has a value, which itself is a document and is enclosed by { }. We will talk about documents in the next chapter in detail.

Besides document ID and properties, a document also has some meta information. This meta information can be viewed from the **Views** console. I will cover the **Views** topic later in *Chapter 6*, *Retrieving Documents without Keys Using Views*. You can view the metadata of a document by transversal to **Web console** | **Views** | **beer-sample** | **Production Views** | **brewery_beers**. The meta information is shown in the following screenshot:

```
beer-sample          ▼ | > Views > | _design/beer/_view/brewery_beers   ▼

▼  green_bay_brewing-hinterland_mild_cask_ale          [Preview a Random Document]  [Edit Document]

{                                                    {
  "name": "Hinterland Mild Cask Ale",                  "id": "green_bay_brewing-
  "abv": 0,                                          hinterland_mild_cask_ale",
  "ibu": 0,                                            "rev": "1-
  "srm": 0,                                          13c356be43bfe5df0000000000000000",
  "upc": 0,                                            "expiration": 0,
  "type": "beer",                                      "flags": 0
  "brewery_id": "green_bay_brewing",                 }
  "updated": "2010-07-22 20:00:20",
  "description": "",
  "style": "English-Style Pale Mild Ale",
  "category": "British Ale"
}
```

The document view

The preceding console provides details about a document, including metadata. Don't worry if you get distracted with the various options provided here. We will come back to this later in *Chapter 6, Retrieving Documents without Keys Using View*.

Keys and metadata

As described earlier, a document key is a unique identifier for a document. The value of a document key can be any string.

In addition to the key, documents usually have three more types of metadata, which are provided by the Couchbase server unless modified by an application developer. They are as follows:

- `rev`: This is an internal revision ID meant for internal use by Couchbase. It should not be used in the application.

- `expiration`: If you want your document to expire after a certain amount of time, you can set that value here. By default, it is 0; that is, the document never expires.

- `flags`: These are numerical values specific to the client library that is updated when the document is stored.

Besides the preceding metadata, a document can also have CAS, a unique identifier associated with a document and used by the Couchbase server to verify whether the document was updated by another process before being deleted or changed. Why do we need this? When we understand APIs, we will explore the need for this attribute to store, delete, and retrieve documents from buckets in *Chapter 5, Introducing Client SDK*.

A document can be of two types:

- **JSON format**: Use this whenever you require a valid form of JSON format
- **Binary data**: Use this whenever you require any data format other than JSON

You have already understood the expiration metadata property. Now let's try to understand how it really works internally to cause data to expire when a developer sets an expiration value to some period of time. There are two ways in which the Couchbase server removes a document from the bucket when a document expiration is set and flagged for deletion. One way is that the key marked for deletion is removed when there is a request for that particular key. This is called **Lazy Deletion**. The other way is if the keys are flagged as expired, then they will be removed by an automatic maintenance process that runs according to the maintenance intervals. By default, this takes place every 60 minutes.

So far, you have understood what a document is and what it consists of, such as the ID, metadata, and so on. Let's try to create a document using the web UI so that you can have some confidence and you can assure others that you too can create a document and not just concepts. Indeed, as an administrator, I have spent a lot of time creating and updating documents whenever there were issues in production and business requirements that demand rectification on priority. Of course, this actions were done with the necessary approval from the business owner. So, let me show you how we can proceed using the web console.

Go to **Data Buckets** | **LearningCouchbase** | **Documents** | **Create Document**, and you will see this:

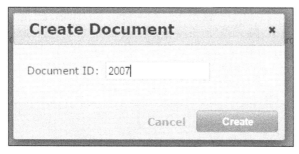

The Document ID console

When you click on **Create Document**, you will be asked to enter the document ID. We have already discussed document ID. Hope you still remember it. But don't worry, you don't need to generate a unique ID in production manually, there are ways to generate a unique ID depending on the client library that will be used to write a document in Couchbase. Then, click on **Create**. Once you click on the **Create** button, you will be shown a console where you can enter the document in the JSON format.

 Ensure that you have enclosed the records properly, or else it will give syntax errors. Most of the time, errors will occur when you forget to enclose brackets properly. It's worth typing it if you have not worked on JSON before.

The document editor

Enter the details as shown in the preceding diagram and save the document. There is no provision to enter metadata other than the document ID in the web console.

You can search the document that you just created using the key only. Hence, you should know the key before you need to retrieve it since the only mechanism to fetch a document is by using the document ID; for the time being, it's the only way. So, you might wonder that a developer needs to remember a million or more keys to retrieve them if we store a lot of documents in a bucket. Not really, luckily Couchbase provides an alternatives mechanism for this. If you have read the first chapter, you can certainly guess what the others ways to retrieve a document from buckets are.

Document view

The other way to retrieve documents without using a document ID is called Views, which we will discuss in *Chapter 6*, *Retrieving Documents without Keys Using Views*. As of now, enter the key, that is, 2007, in the textbox provided to the left of the **Lookup Id** button, and click on it. You will see details of the document, as follows:

The document editor

vBuckets

Now you are able to create a bucket and store documents in it. So, let's try to understand another concept, vBucket, which helps in replicating documents across the nodes in a cluster, before moving to the next chapter. In order to understand vBucket, you need to understand document ID, which we already discussed. It is a unique key per bucket, that is associated with each document. Whenever an application needs to store a document in a bucket, it needs to be associated with a unique key, just as a primary key does in the RDBMS table.

Depending on the document ID, documents are distributed across the nodes in a cluster. Each bucket is divided into 1024 logical partitions which are called **vBucket**. Each partition is bound to a particular node in the cluster. This bindings of vBucket to server nodes is stored in a cluster map, which is a lookup structure. Each vBucket will have a subset of document IDs. This mechanism allows effective distribution and sharding of documents across the nodes in a cluster.

 Whenever we configure replications using replicas, in a bucket, it is the vBucket that allows movement of documents from one node to another. Also, it is vBucket that gets replicated across the cluster. It is not created by the administrator; it's managed internally by the Couchbase cluster.

So far, we have discussed that a Couchbase cluster consists of multiple nodes and documents are distributed across the cluster using vBucket. But how does a node know which documents or vBuckets in which it is mapped to? The Couchbase client derives the node using a hashing algorithm for each document it stores. This hashing function algorithm takes the document ID for each document and returns the vBucket in which it belongs to and refers to the cluster map to determine the node to store the actual document in. The client uses this information to communicate with the node directly to store or retrieve the document. The following diagram shows a mapping from a document ID to vBuckets using the hash function:

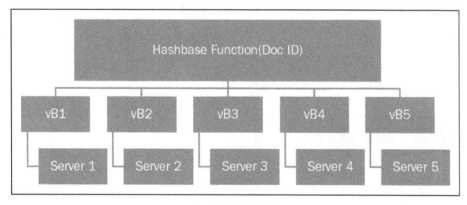

The vBucket map

In this example, there are three server nodes in the cluster, and they are represented by the leaf nodes. Whenever a client wants to store a document in a bucket with a given document ID, the client library hashes the key and determines the vBucket to which it belongs using the hash algorithm. Then, this vBucket is used to look up in the mapping table, cluster map that consists of mapping entry for each vBucket to a server node. After that, the client directly communicates with the server node and stores the data. The same process is followed for all other operations, such as get, update, and so on.

For example, let's say that we want to store a document with a document ID, 2007. This ID will be passed as an input parameter to the hash function and returns a vBucket say, vB4. Using this vBucket, vB4, the client refers to the cluster map to determine the server in which this particular vBucket resides, say Server 2 in our case. A particular vBucket can belong to only one server in a cluster at a time. The number of vBuckets will be determined by Couchbase for better manageability. By design, Couchbase splits each bucket into 1,024 vBuckets, and these vBuckets are evenly distributed across nodes in the cluster. Administrators don't have any role in specifying the number of vBuckets. Let me show you how to determine the numbers of vBuckets in our environment now.

Go to **Server Nodes | 127.0.0.1 | Select bucket (beer-sample) | vBucket Resources**, and you will see this:

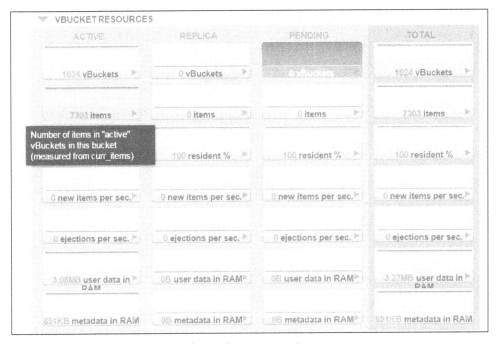

The vBucket resources view

Do not be overwhelmed by seeing a lot of metrics in the preceding diagram. To determine information about each of these metrics, you simply need to hover the mouse over it. It will display descriptions of each metric as shown previously. They are all self-explanatory.

Understanding some internals of Couchbase

Let's understand some of the internal concepts of the Couchbase cluster. It will help you to determine the ideal value for various parameters for fine-tuning Couchbase, when we look at tuning in *Chapter 10*, *Administration, Tuning, and Monitoring*.

Ejection

Before we conclude the chapter, let's understand some concepts about internal workings of Couchbase. We will discuss how performance is provided in Couchbase, the replication process, protocol usage, and so on.

As discussed earlier, Couchbase ensures that the most frequently accessed data is stored in the RAM, which is an inbuilt caching layer, and boosts performance, but eventually flushes data to disks for persistence. However, if all the data needs to be stored only in the RAM, then the cluster will require a lot of memory. Thus, to hold large amount of data, Couchbase flushes documents out of the memory to accommodate incoming documents. This process flushes the document to the disk before removing it from the memory. Thus, it allows storage of more data than the memory capacity.

Movement of data between the RAM and disks is automatically performed asynchronously by Couchbase, ensuring that the most frequently used information or documents are stored in the memory and only the least used data is removed from the memory. This process of removing data from the memory when it can't hold incoming documents from the client is called **ejection**; the threshold for ejection can be configured for each bucket and controlled by the cluster.

Although data gets ejected from the memory when the threshold is reached, metadata that holds information for each document stored in the bucket is held in the RAM all the time, thus allowing the server to determine whether a document ID is present or not from the memory itself before fetching documents from the disk storage. However, to return the whole document to the client, it can retrieve a document from either the RAM or the disk, depending on the availability of the document in the RAM or not. By default, this process of moving information to the disk is performed asynchronously by the cluster.

While documents are being ejected to the disk from the memory in the background process, the server continues to service requests from clients. Sometimes, due to high write operations on buckets, clients will be notified by Couchbase that the server is temporarily unable to handle writes because of an out-of-memory problem, until enough documents have been ejected from the memory to the disk.

Warmup

A warmup is a process that loads data from the disk to the RAM, making documents available for client requests when the Couchbase server is restarted or when it is started after restoration from backup. Client requests can be serviced by Couchbase only after the completion of this process. The time taken to warm up a cluster for loading data into the memory depends on the size of the data, number of nodes, and configuration of the cluster.

 If the warmup is taking a lot of time in your cluster, then you can change the total percentage of RAM to be filled by documents in the warmup process using the `cbepctl ep_warmup_min_memory_threshold` parameter.

Replication

Replication is configured per bucket, and at most, you can configure up to three replicas only. These replicas work closely with the vBucket structure and cluster map. Replicas of individual vBuckets distribute documents across the cluster. Distribution of replicas within the cluster ensures that a single point of failure is prevented. Replication of this data within the cluster is entirely peer-to-peer-based, with information being exchanged directly between nodes in the cluster. When data is written to a node within the cluster, it is logically partitioned in one of the vBuckets and then distributed to one or more nodes, depending on the replication factor, as a replica vBucket simultaneously.

Whenever there is a failure of one of the nodes in the cluster, replica vBuckets are converted to an active vBucket in place of the vBuckets that failed because of the node failure. This process occurs instantaneously. A failover can be performed manually, or a built-in automatic failover can be used. An automatic failover is also called a hard failover, which immediately fails over a node and might lead to data loss.

When a node within a cluster becomes unavailable, the failover process contacts all nodes that are acting as a replica for the failed node, and converts the replica vBucket to an active vBucket from one of the replica nodes and updates the internal table and cluster map to enable the client to send requests for a document to the available server.

Replicas are configured on each bucket. Hence, this allows an administrator to configure different buckets to have a different number of replicas, according to the importance of the business requirement.

> Replicas are only enabled once the number of nodes within the cluster supports the required number of replicas. This means that, when you configure two replicas on a bucket, the cluster will enable it only when it has three nodes, or else it will give you a warning message as shown in the following screenshot. You can view alerts from the server and bucket settings of the web UI.

Server settings

The server settings are as follows:

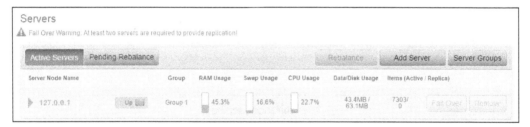

The server nodes view

Bucket settings

These are the bucket settings to enable replicas. You will get a warning message when the cluster doesn't have enough nodes to replicate a document.

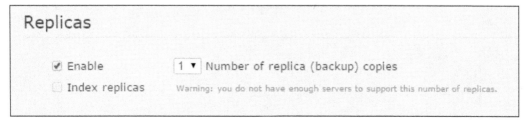

The replicas setting

Rebalancing

By now, you have understood that documents are stored within a Couchbase server through a distribution mechanism offered by the vBucket structure. If administrators need to expand or shrink the Couchbase server cluster to increase or downsize its capacity, which is very common in the cloud environment for elasticity, then the information stored in vBuckets needs to be redistributed between the available nodes with a process called rebalancing, in which the corresponding vBucket cluster map is updated to reflect the new structure.

One thing that needs to be kept in mind as an administrator is that you need to initiate rebalancing manually when the cluster structure changes.

When an administrator adds or removes a node from the cluster, they can rebalance the cluster data using the **Rebalance** button, which is shown in the next screenshot. It is grayed out right now, since no rebalancing is required in our case. The button will be enabled when there is a pending rebalance.

The rebalancing setting

The rebalancing process can take place while the cluster is running and servicing requests. During rebalancing, data is moved in the background process across the replica nodes. Clients can read and write to the existing structure without any disturbance. Once the process of moving is complete, the vBucket cluster map is updated and communicated to the clients. The protocol that is used internally in Couchbase to exchange data throughout the system is called the **TAP protocol**.

TAP is used during replication of documents between nodes to satisfy the replicas' requirement. It is also used during the procedure of rebalancing within a cluster to move data and redistribute information across the nodes in a cluster. The details of TAP can be viewed using the web UI console, as shown in the following screenshot. Hover the mouse over each attribute to view its details.

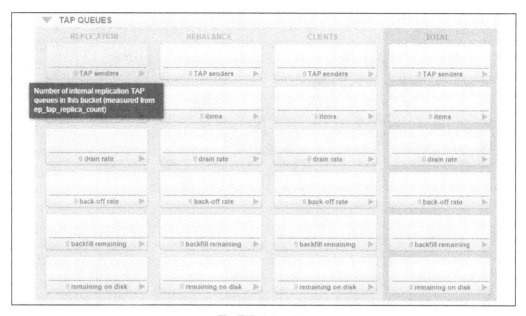

The TAP status view

Summary

In this chapter, you learned how to create a bucket. We explored the concepts of documents and the mechanism of data storage in the Couchbase cluster. Next, we saw some internal mechanisms of Couchbase, such as ejection, replication, warmup, rebalancing, and so on.

In the next chapter, we will explore documents in detail and review some of the design considerations that need to be kept in mind while designing a document in Couchbase.

4
Designing a Document for Couchbase

The chapter will introduce the concepts of JSON, compare NoSQL with RDBMS, and explain how to manage relationships between various documents. It will also familiarize you with the document editor option so that you can create and edit a document using the web UI. We will try to understand the various ways of designing a document for a Couchbase cluster. Earlier, we specified that the developer doesn't need to worry about the schema. However, while developing any application, we do need some kind of schema modeling to provide a coherent schema and represent domain objects, though nothing as stringent as an RDBMS table structure.

Understanding JSON and non JSON data

Let's try to understand the representation of a document in Couchbase. A document in Couchbase can be represented by JSON as well as by non JSON binary data. We have already explored the JSON format in an earlier chapter, and now you might be wondering why I am trying to explain it further. When you design a document for storage and retrieval from Couchbase, you will be working extensively in the JSON format. Hence, understanding it in detail is very important when it comes to designing documents for performance and efficiency.

JSON is a text format that is completely language-independent and a lightweight data interchange format. It is built on two structures, as follows:

- A collection of name and value pairs: Depending on the type of language, it can be realized as an object, record, dictionary, hash table, keyed list, or associative array

- An ordered list of values: This is represented as an array, vector, or list

Its representation is quite similar to that of JavaScript.

A document representation of a shopping cart in the JSON format for an e-commerce application is shown here:

```
{
    "book"  :  "Learning Couchbase",
    "isbn"  :  "978-1-78528-859-3",
    "price": 21.30,
    "quantity": 2,
    "active": true,
    "expire": "2015/06/10 9:12:10",
    "types": ["ebook","print"]
}
```

A JSON document

The preceding JSON document represents a shopping cart entry. A JSON document enables representation of complex documents with ease and in a human-readable format. As you just saw, we can easily determine that there is an attribute called `"book"` and its value is `"Learning Couchbase"`. Likewise, the `"types"` attribute specifies that this particular book is available in both e-book and print formats.

There are some data types that are supported by JSON. In the preceding code, book and isbn are of the string data type and are represented by values within double quotes (" "). They can also be surrounded by single quotes. Any value without quotes is treated as numeric, such as the price and quantity attributes. The types attribute belongs to an array data type. It can be a collection of objects or documents. Attributes such as book and isbn are called **keys**. In our example, these are string values such as `"Learning Couchbase"` and `"978-1-78528-859-3"` that are the respective values of the keys and can be of any data type discussed so far.

A shopping cart – understanding data types

Let's try to map field types of the document that was described earlier, although the types are not specified in the document. They are implicit in nature and are represented as follows:

Field	Type	Value
book	String	Learning Couchbase
isbn	String	978-1-78528-859-3
price	numeric	21.30
quantity	numeric	2
active	boolean	true

Field	Type	Value
expireOn	Time Stamp	2015/06/10 9:12:10
types	Arrays	["ebook","print"]

So, you can clearly observe that, without declaring any types along with the data, you can infer the type of each attribute from the nature of the value; for example, any value within double quotes (""") is a `string`. A JSON document is a logical container of data and it represents data as a row entry does in an RDBMS table. However, the main difference is that JSON represents a comprehensive document, which is self-completed in nature, that is, it contains the entire information required to represent an entity in a single document without any normalization; whereas in RDBMS, you split it into multiple tables for preserving the data space.

Couchbase can also store documents in binary that can't be represented in the JSON format. If you want to store files such as PDF or MS Word documents, then you can store them as binary data. Fetching documents by clients will be performant since requests will be served from the memory itself.

Document versus RDBMS

Before you understand the various considerations that need to be kept in mind while designing a document for any document-based system, particularly a Couchbase system, let me explain what a document really is and how it differs from RDBMS.

Often during my training sessions, participants have asked me what a document is really all about. They are often confused about document files, such as `.pdf` or `.doc` file formats. This terminology doesn't represent a file as you perceive in software world. Here, "document" means representation of information as perceived in reality or in the physical world. In reality, when we represent information, we discuss or represent it as a single complete document without breaking it into multiple documents and linking them to each other. For example, when we represent an invoice document, there are different sections, such as invoice, address, and items. If you need to store a domain object in a document, it will be represented as whole information, and this is good from application perspective as well since the whole information is encapsulated in a single document format. Documents are represented in the JSON format for clarity and ease of understanding. It also stores metadata of the information along with the document itself. The document is mapped to an object in your application directly without denormalizing it into different tables as we do in RDBMS.

In case of the RDBMS systems, we store records in a table and each row represents a document. We normalize information or data into various tables to save space. When we normalize information by splitting it across various tables, we are creating complexities for retrieving the whole information since the database engine needs to consolidate it with a `joins` query from various tables. This is the main cause of deteriorating performance in most applications, since joins can be expensive in terms of system resources, that is, CPU, RAM usage, and so on.

Here is a table that differentiates between a document and RDBMS:

Document	RDBMS
It's schemaless	A schema needs to be defined in terms of table structures
Metadata about the attributes goes, or is stored, with the data itself	Records are stored individually and without attributes
Atomicity is for a single document only	This supports ACID properties
No joins are allowed between documents	Joins are supported across tables
Transactions are on a single document only	Most modern RDBMSs support transactions
This is good for structured and unstructured data	Good for structured data
This can handle big data without much cost	Handling big data is expensive

Document modeling

In order to bring agility to applications that change business processes frequently demanded by its business environment, being schemaless is a good feature. In this methodology, you don't need to be concerned about structures of data initially while designing the application. This means as a developer, you don't need to worry about structures of a database schema, such as tables, or splitting information into various tables; instead, you should focus on application requirement and satisfying business needs.

I still recollect various moments related to design domain objects/tables, which I went through when I was a developer, especially the time when I had just graduated from engineering college and was into developing applications for a corporate. Whenever I was a part of any application requirement discussion, I always had these questions at the back of my mind:

- How does a domain object get stored in the database?

- What will the table structures be?

- How will I retrieve the domain objects?

- Will it be difficult to use ORM, such as Hibernate, Ejb, and so on?

My point here is that, instead of being mentally present in the discussion on requirement gathering and understanding the business requirements in detail, I spent more time mapping business entities in a table format. The reason was that, if I did not put forward the technical constraints at that time, it would be difficult to revert later about the technical challenges we could face in the data structure design.

Earlier, whenever we talked about application design, we always thought about database design structures, such as converting objects into multiple tables using normalization forms (2NF/3NF), and spent a lot of time mapping database objects to application objects using various ORM tools, such as Hibernate, Ejb, and so on. In document modeling, we will always think in terms of application requirements, that is, data or information flow while designing documents, not in terms of storage. We can simply start our application development using business representation of an entity without much concern about the storage structures. Having covered the various advantages provided by a document-based system, in this section we will discuss how to design such kind of documents, which can be stored in any document-based database system, such as Couchbase. Then, we can effectively design domain objects for coherence with the application requirements.

 Whenever we model a document's structure, we need to consider two main points; storing all information in one document and breaking it down into multiple documents. You need to consider these and choose one, keeping the application requirements, in mind.

So, an important factor is to evaluate whether the information contains unrelated data components, which are independent and can be broken up into different documents or all the components that represent a complete domain object, which could be accessed together most of the time. If data components in the information are related and will be required most of the time in a business logic, consider grouping them as a single logical container so that the application developer won't perceive them as separate objects or documents. All of these factors depend on the nature of the application being developed and its use cases. Besides these, you need to think in terms of accessing information, such as atomicity, single unit of access, and so on. You can ask yourself question such as, "Are we going to create or modify the information as a single unit or not?". You also need to consider concurrency, what will happen when the document is accessed by multiple clients at the same time, and so on.

After looking at all these considerations that you need to keep in mind while designing a document, you have two options: one is to keep all of the information in a single document, and the other is to have a separate document for every different object type.

When all of the related information is stored in a single document, sometimes there will be repetition of data. For example, in an e-commerce order system, if we store addresses of a customer along with each order in a single document and if we have multiple orders for a single consumer, the address details will be repetitive for each order. What will happen in this case? We will have redundant data in terms of storing address in repetition for each order created by the customer. However, data storage is not a major concern nowadays, and this methodology will provide better performance since we don't require any join of documents and will be fetching all information; both order and address as a single unit all the time. It can also scale out easily since all related information is stored in a single document. Thus, the need for client-side joins is eliminated, since all of the information is stored physically together. This option is the easiest, since all of the related information is included in a single document.

In contrast to the single document strategy, we can also have separate documents for objects that are different in nature instead of consolidating them in a single document. There are some points you need to keep in mind while opting for this particular option. Since information is decentralized into different documents, related objects might not be co-located. If business logic requires these multiple documents for a particular reason, it might require retrieving documents from different nodes while being used in the application. Couchbase doesn't support joins, so if there is a need to fetch all the documents for the business logic, it requires multiple fetches from Couchbase and the application logic needs to be written to consolidate it. Moreover, there is no support for transactions across documents; atomicity is by definition for a single document only. If there is a need to perform joins on multiple documents, then this needs to be taken care of by the client side application only. These are few considerations you need to keep in mind while designing documents in Couchbase.

In the next section, let me provide a checklist that will enable you to take a decision on whether to break an information or business object into multiple documents or have a single document in your application.

One document versus multiple documents

Many a times when we design documents for the Couchbase system, we have two options: either a single document or multiple documents. The following table will help you make an appropriate choice for your specific use case:

One document	Multiple documents
This is in a denormalized data format, in which all information is stored together in a single document	Information will be split into multiple documents thereby normalizing data
This leads to better performance since all of the information is kept together	There is an impact on the performance, since related documents are scattered across nodes
You don't need to join a document since all related information is at a single document	Join is not supported, while the application logic requires it

Before taking a decision on which options to go ahead with, always keep in mind how information will be grouped logically in your application.

Whatever we discussed is applicable to any document-based system. Now let's try to explore in depth the details specific to a Couchbase cluster. Whatever we discussed holds true for Couchbase. However, we need to consider some additional points for a document specific to Couchbase, such as the key.

We need to choose a document ID, or key, wisely, since all the documents are sharded across the nodes within a cluster based on the document ID only. It's this document ID that is used in a hash function to determine the node for storing a particular document. It's the same as the primary key of a table in a relational database system. The document ID should be unique in a bucket—it's mandatory. The bucket won't allow you to add a document whose document ID is already present in the bucket.

 You, as a developer, need to ensure that no two documents have the same document ID. For the time being, don't worry about this, since there are a lot of mechanisms for generating unique IDs, such as UUID. It all depends on the client API.

We will cover various mechanisms for generating unique IDs later, when I explain how an API interacts with Couchbase in *Chapter 5, Introducing Client SDK*. By default, a document in a bucket can be retrieved using the document ID only. There are, however, other ways of retrieving a document, such as views, which we will discuss in the following chapter. Retrieving a document from the Couchbase bucket using the document ID is extremely fast; by using the document ID, the client determines the nodes in which the document is stored using the consistent hash function, and retrieves the document directly from the memory if it is present in the memory itself. Otherwise, it is retrieved from the disk, provided the document has already been flushed to the disk storage. Care must be taken in choosing document IDs, since they can't be changed at a later stage, as there is no provision to update them.

Suppose you have an application logic that needs to differentiate between various records or documents using the business requirement or some attributes of data — say, in an e-commerce application; users need to have different consumer IDs. You can have all the registered users assigned a unique consumer ID generated by the application logic. Then it's best to choose an attribute as a document ID that can be use to retrieve documents directly. A key can be generated using UUID, depending on the client APIs used to access the Couchbase cluster. My experience indicates that it is best to use unique values of the business entity when choosing the document ID; for example, when we have an e-mail ID in the business entity, for users it's better to have the e-mail ID as the document ID for our e-commerce application. Since an e-mail ID is always unique, it will be an ideal candidate for use as a document ID for such use cases.

Let's try to understand both (single and multiple documents) of these options for an e-commerce model in which there will be two sets of information: customers and order. An e-commerce data model is a very huge and complex model, so for the sake of this discussion, without complicating it, we will discuss only these two entities. As discussed earlier, we have two options, **single** and **multiple** documents. Let me show them to you one after the other. If we have to design using a single document, then it can be represented as shown in the following screenshot. It maintains all the related information in a single document.

```
{
    "name": "Henderson P",
    "user_id": "hendersonp",
    "email_id": "hendersonp@ht.com",
    "password": "#!2007.CP:"
    "order": {
        "order_id": 2015051527
        "shipping": {
            "address": "Chingamakha",
            "city": "Imphal",
            "landmark": "Nr Tomal Lane",
            "state": "MN",
            "country": "India",
            "delivery_instruction": "Deliver between 5 to 6. PM only",
        },
        "payment": {
            "method": "COD",
            "transaction_id": "20070327"
        },
    "products": [
            {"quantity": 4, "sku":"978-1-78528-859-3", "title": "Learning Couchbase", "unit_cost":4500}
            ]
    }

    }
```

Order - JSON document

The preceding document represents an order store along with the consumer details in a single document. The order itself is a document, as it is enclosed by { } and the products value is an array represented by [ ].

Hold on! Have you gone through the order document, shown previously? If not, spend sometime more and observe it carefully.

What did you observe? Was there any redundant information?

If the business process, that is, the order process for this particular use case, discussed previously and represented by the order document allows multiple orders per user and the shipping addresses, represented by the shipping attribute in the order document, is the same as the permanent address, then whenever there is a new order for the same consumer, the shipping address will always be repeated per order for each user. So, there might be some redundancy in data for such cases.

The main advantage of this kind of design is that all of the information is encapsulated in a single document, hence it's easy to retrieve the information in one operation. We don't need to worry about joins, transactions, and so on. If you remember earlier discussion on atomicity, atomicity is maintained per document. So, when we include all of the related information or data in one document, everything is in one document, hence atomicity is taken care of by Couchbase itself. Couchbase ensures that a single document will be always stored as a whole and never partially. However, there is one issue in such a scenario. Even if your application does not require displaying order details, whenever we fetch this document to access the user details, it will always fetch the orders details as well.

Sometimes, it will be heavy if we have a lot of items in order details and we require user details frequently but order details are not required. So, you should be very careful while designing a document. As a thumb rule, always design documents as per the needs of the application's logic as a data flow.

What is the other alternative? One alternative is to split the information into multiple documents. In our case, we can split the information into two documents. One document will represent user details, and the other document will represent order details. When we split information into multiple documents, we need to find a mechanism to link these two documents. You will understand that in the next section.

User

Let's represent the domain objects, Order, and the user as a separate documents as shown here:

```
{
    "name": "Henderson P",
    "user_id": "hendersonp",
    "email_id": "hendersonp@ht.com",
    "password": "#!2007.CP:"

}
```

The user object

Order

The domain object, order is represented in the JSON format as shown here:

```
{
    "consumer_logon":"hendersonp",
    "order_id": 2015051527,
    "shipping": {
        "address": "Chingamakha",
        "city": "Imphal",
        "landmark": "Nr Tomal Lane",
        "state": "MN",
        "country": "India",
        "delivery_instruction": "Deliver between 5 to 6. PM only"
    },
    "payment": {
        "method": "COD",
        "transaction_id": "20070327"
    },
    "products": [
        {"quantity": 4, "sku":"978-1-78528-859-3",
                    "title": "Learning Couchbase", "unit_cost":4500}
    ]

}
```

Order

When we split information into multiple documents, we normalize information that removes redundancy of data. However, you should keep in mind that disk space should not be a constraint in a distributed system such as the NoSQL database system, since nowadays HDDs are cheaper and Couchbase works well in a commodity servers. The point, is if redundancy provides performance and eases your development, then you should opt for it. This design requires you, as a developer, in application code to take care of retrieving order details (in the application code) along with the user document, just in case you need to display both documents for a particular use case. Since there is no join of documents in Couchbase, you need two fetch operations for it: one for the user document and the other for the order document. Furthermore, you can remove the address information from order details. There are a lot of ways to design it. Whenever you design a document, always think in terms of the application logic's requirement to satisfy business needs. Think of a document as a logical container for an entity, and then think of how to group relevant information together.

You also need to consider the document ID/key selection while designing a document. As discussed earlier, it is the same as the primary key and has to be unique for each document in a bucket. All documents are sharded based on the document ID across the nodes within a cluster. So, what options do we have for the document ID? You can use system-generated UUIDs or application-related values.

 A **universally unique identifier** (**UUID**) is an identifier standard used in software construction. A UUID is simply a 128-bit value. The meaning of each bit is defined by any of several variants.

Document relationships

In a document-based database system, such as Couchbase, you don't need to worry about altering tables when there are changes in the schema, as we usually have to do in RDBMS. All schemas of a document are driven by application code only. Whenever there is a need to change schema, we don't need to worry much, as schema of a document goes along with the document itself as metadata. We don't need to change any schema explicitly at the bucket level. We just need to think about the latency, update, and read pattern of documents in terms of dataflow while designing document. We will be more concerned about data flow than data storage. However, my experience leads me to feel, that if you can design a document as a standalone entity, that's the best thing.

We have seen two ways of designing documents: one that includes all related information in one document and others splitting information into multiple documents. If we have to choose the second option, there should be a way to link the related documents. Let's try to understand how we can link between documents.

User and Order

How do we maintain a relationship between the two domain objects, user and order? Let me show you in this section.

```
{
    "name": "Henderson P",
    "user_id": "hendersonp",
    "email_id": "hendersonp@ht.com",
    "password": "#!2007.CP:"

}
            {
                "consumer_logon":"hendersonp",
                "order_id": 2015051527,
                "shipping": {
                    "address": "Chingamakha",
                    "city": "Imphal",
                    "landmark": "Nr Tomal Lane",
                    "state": "MN",
                    "country": "India",
                    "delivery_instruction": "Deliver between 5 to 6. PM only"
                },
                "payment": {
                    "method": "COD",
                    "transaction_id": "20070327"
                },
                "products": [
                    {"quantity": 4, "sku":"978-1-78528-859-3",
                                "title": "Learning Couchbase", "unit_cost":4500}
                ]

            }
```

User to-order relationship

As shown in the preceding screenshot, you can store the user_id value of user document in the Order document; which is shown as the consumer_logon attribute in our example. In this way, you can retrieve all orders of a particular user ID using consumer_logon. Likewise, you can also retrieve user documents from the order using the consumer_logon attribute. Suppose you want to determine the user for a particular order. You can use the consumer_logon attribute of the order to fetch the corresponding user document, provided the user_id attribute value is the document ID for that user document. Otherwise, you can create a view to retrieve it, which we will discuss in *Chapter 6, Retrieving Documents without Keys Using Views*.

Using the document editor

Let's familiarize ourselves with the document editor provided in the Couchbase admin console. Let's create the document that was just discussed using the document editor. Make sure that you store the user and order documents as defined in the bucket, LearningCouchbase that we created earlier.

User

You can enter the **User** document using the document editor of the web console, as shown here:

```
LearningCouchbase        ▾  > Documents

200703                                          Delete   Save As   Save

1  {
2     "name": "Henderson P",
3     "user_id": "hendersonp",
4     "email_id": "hendersonp@ht.com",
5     "password": "#!2007.CP:"
6  }
```

The User document

Order

Just like **User**, enter the **Order** details as follows. Make sure that you select the **LearningCouchbase** bucket.

```
LearningCouchbase        ▾  > Documents

2015051527                                       Delete   Save As   Save

1  {
2     "consumer_logon": "hendersonp",
3     "order_id": 2015051527,
4     "shipping": {
5        "address": "Chingamakha",
6        "city": "Imphal",
7        "landmark": "Nr Tomal Lane",
8        "state": "MN",
9        "country": "India",
10       "delivery_instruction": "Deliver between 5 to 6. PM only"
11    },
12    "payment": {
13       "method": "COD",
14       "transaction_id": "20070327"
15    },
16    "products": [
17       {
18          "quantity": 6,
19          "sku": "978-1-78528-859-3",
20          "title": "Learning Couchbase",
21          "unit_cost": 4500
22       }
23    ]
24 }
```

Order document

Now you know how to create a document using the document editor. Let me explain how you can update an attribute, say `quantity`, in the order document. Go to the **LearningCouchbase** bucket's document display list, as shown in the following screenshot. Key in its document ID, which is `2015051527`, in the **Lookup Id** textbox, and click on the **Lookup Id** button.

Documents

Change the quantity from `6` to `8` and save it as follows:

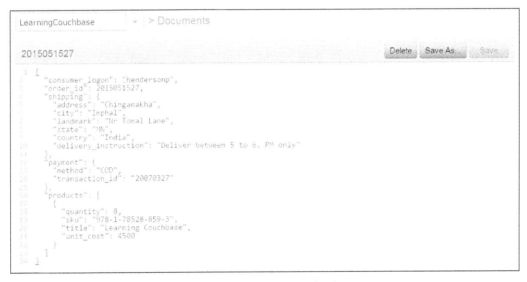

The document editor - updating order document

This completes the modeling of documents to be stored in the Couchbase system.

Summary

In this chapter, we took a brief overview of documents and how to model a document for a particular business requirement. We also discussed some important design considerations for maintaining relationships between various documents. In addition to that, we discussed the difference between documents and RDBMS. Finally, you learned to use the document editor and create and edit a document using the web console.

In the next chapter, you will understand how to connect to Couchbase using the Java API, and we will cover various operations that can be performed with it.

5
Introducing Client SDK

In this chapter, we will provide an overview of the various client APIs that connect to Couchbase. Conceptually, we will understand the various methods that are available for interacting with Couchbase. These are applicable to most client APIs irrespective of the programming language you choose to develop your applications. Finally, we will introduce APIs specific to Java SDK 2.1. This chapter will also explain the concept behind counters and locking mechanisms that are provided by the Couchbase SDK APIs. Next, you will learn about the features that are used to connect asynchronously and working with the Observable class. We can also use this feature to determine the presence of a specific document in the Couchbase storage, asynchronously. Finally, towards the end of the chapter, we will discuss connection management provided by the client SDK.

By the end of this chapter, you will be able to write applications that connect to Couchbase and perform various CRUD operations using Java APIs.

A Couchbase SDK overview

So far, in the previous chapters, we have understood how to create buckets and store documents in them using the bucket editor via the web admin console. We have also discussed some of the guidelines used for designing document-based database systems.

What if we need to connect and perform operations on the Couchbase cluster from an application? This can be achieved using the Couchbase client libraries, which are also collectively known as Couchbase **Software Development Kit** (**SDK**). The Couchbase SDK APIs are language dependent. The concepts remain the same and are applicable to all languages that are supported by the SDK. However, there are some features such as thread safe, asynchronous operations, and so on that are language dependent. For example, thread safe features are tested and certified for Java SDK and .NET SDK, version 1.0 and above.

You can refer to the Couchbase website (`http://docs.couchbase.com/developer/dev-guide-3.0/thread-safety.html`) for further details about SDKs other than the Java SDK.

Let's now discuss Couchbase APIs as a concept without referring to any specific language, and then we will map these concepts to Java APIs in the Java SDK section. Couchbase SDK clients are also known as smart clients since they understand the overall status of the cluster, that is, cluster map, to keep information about the vBucket and its server nodes updated. There are two types of Couchbase clients:

- **Smart clients**: Such clients can understand the health of the cluster and receive constant updates about the information of the cluster. Each smart client maintains a cluster map that can derive the cluster node where a document is stored using the document ID. Examples are Java, .NET, and so on.

- **Memcached compatible**: Such clients are used for applications that will interact with traditional memcached buckets, which are not aware of vBucket. It needs to install Moxi (a memcached proxy) on all clients that require access to the Couchbase memcache bucket, which acts as a proxy to convert the API's call to the memcache compatible call.

Having understood types of Couchbase clients, and before going into the details of APIs, let's get a better understanding of applying Couchbase APIs in general. We will discuss how read and write operations work in Couchbase. This will give you more insights into why we need to perform some operations in a specific manner. In any RDBMS, whenever we need to insert a record into a table, we execute an `INSERT` command and wait for an acknowledgement that the record is stored in the disk; this provides durability. However, in Couchbase, all documents get stored in RAM, and the server will confirm that a write is successful as soon as it gets stored in RAM, which is volatile in nature. This may not be appropriate for your application; you may require the documents to be stored in the disk for durability. Couchbase APIs provide all of these options as configurable parameters. Thus, you need to understand the internal workings of Couchbase read and write well to use these APIs properly.

We need to unlearn and forgo some of RDBMS database concepts such as normalization, foreign key, and so on, which you learned when you developed applications based on a traditional RDBMS. For example, we design data fetching operations in such a way that a single operation will fetch as many records as possible in one hop, that is, by retrieving data using joins on multiple tables to avoid accessing database tables frequently. We design like this because fetching records from database tables is costly in terms of resource utilization, and fetching records from disk storage is not always recommended as connecting to databases consume resources.

You also need to remember that RDBMS is designed to store and retrieve data efficiently. However, performance bottlenecks always arise whenever there are multiple joins across multiple tables, no matter which RDBMS you choose for data storage or which design you follow.

In contrast to this, Couchbase recommends to fetch only the required information at a time instead of fetching all records in one hop, since fetching data using the get commands with the document ID is very fast. This is fast since most of these records are present in the memory. Hence, whenever we need to retrieve documents from the Couchbase cluster, we should fetch only the essential documents that are required at that instance for the logic, instead of fetching all records in one read for subsequent processing. This is the approach that you need to keep in mind while fetching documents from the Couchbase cluster.

Before exploring various operations using Couchbase APIs, let's understand some basic operation rules followed by the Couchbase server. Some rules of thumb that you need to keep in mind while developing Couchbase application are as follows:

- Whenever you need to perform any operation on the Couchbase cluster, you will require a document key. Couchbase ensures that all operations are atomic as long as all items are on a single document.

- There is no implicit locking of documents. However, Couchbase SDK APIs provide a mechanism to perform locking using GETL, which will be explained later in the chapter.

Understanding write operation in the Couchbase cluster

Let's see how the write operation works in the Couchbase cluster. When a write command is issued using the set operation in the Couchbase cluster, the server immediately responds once the document is written to the memory of that particular node. How do clients know which nodes in the cluster will be responsible for storing the document? You might recall that every operation requires a document ID, using this document ID, the hash algorithm determines the vBucket in which it belongs. Then, this vBucket is used to determine the node that will store the document. All mapping information, vBucket to node, is stored in each of the Couchbase client SDKs, which form the cluster map. The Couchbase client library polls cluster to update the cluster map information all the time.

After the node has responded to the write operation, the Couchbase node puts a copy of the document in the disk queue to flush the document to the disk for durability. If you have configured the bucket for replication, then another copy of the document also gets pushed into a replication queue to replicate to other nodes within a cluster. All of these operations of flushing to queues happen asynchronously.

 You need to keep in mind that the Couchbase client doesn't wait for documents to get stored in the disk. You should take the utmost care because some documents will get lost if they do not persist on the disk.

Suppose, while writing document to Couchbase, the node confirms that the write is done after storing document in the RAM and before persisting it on the disk or replicating it to another node. If that particular node crashed at that very moment, your document would be lost. This is definitely not what you want. Hence, client SDKs provide options to wait until the document gets persisted on the disk. For this, we need to supply a flag and wait until it gets stored on the disk. However, this will impact the response latency. So, you should take a call and decide to go for persistency or performance, depending on your application requirement. We will see the actual method signature and syntax of read and write methods when we discuss Java APIs, later in this chapter.

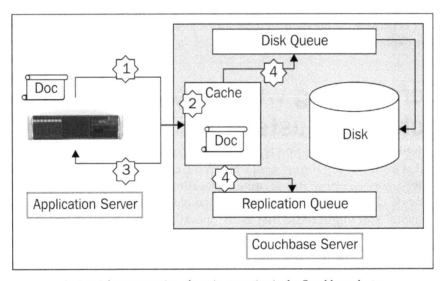

A pictorial representation of a write operation in the Couchbase cluster

Understanding update operations in the Couchbase cluster

An update operation behaves in a sequence similar to that of a write operation. If the document is already present in the RAM, it updates the document in the memory and acknowledges that the update was successful. Otherwise, it will retrieve the document that matches the document ID from storage and update it in the memory.

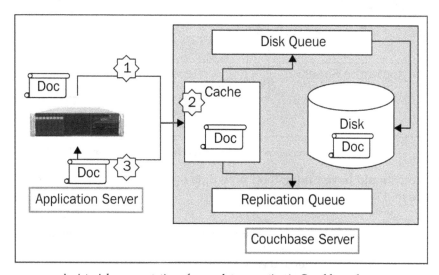

A pictorial representation of an update operation in Couchbase cluster

Understanding read operation in the Couchbase cluster

What about retrieving documents using a read operation—using the document ID? The Couchbase server will look for documents in the memory and return them directly from the memory. However, if the document was flushed and not present in the memory, the Couchbase server will retrieve the document from the disk and store it in the memory.

After that, the read operation will serve the document from the memory to the client.

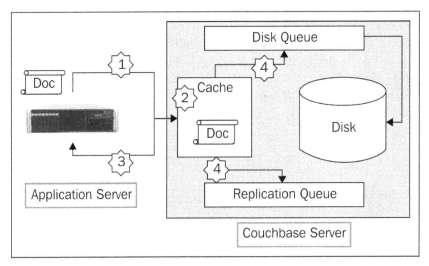

A pictorial representation of a read operation in the Couchbase cluster

By now, you should have understood how data operations ensue under the hood in Couchbase.

One important thing you need to remember is that, although documents are distributed evenly using vBuckets across servers within a cluster and each server maintains both active and replica documents, only one document is active at a time. The client library provides a simple interface to interact with the Couchbase cluster with ease, and provides the latest and updated cluster map to map documents to the vBucket and then to the node or server of a cluster.

Multiple clients on various application servers can access the same document at the same time. However, there is no concept of locking in Couchbase. If you need this facility, you will have to take care of it in your application itself. We will discuss this later in the locking section of this chapter.

While performing any operation on the Couchbase cluster, you must know the document ID or key. No operation can be performed without the document ID unless you use views or N1QL. Usually, document keys are strings and are enclosed by quotes for any client SDK. You can't have space between key values. The value for a document can be a string or any object that is serializable.

Which are the supported smart clients? There are various smart clients that are officially supported by Couchbase. Some of the widely used smart clients are Java, .NET, PHP, Ruby, C, Python, and so on. We will subsequently explore the Java SDK 2.1 in some detail. You can download this SDK from `http://packages.couchbase.com/clients/java/2.1.3/Couchbase-Java-Client-2.1.3.zip`.

You can also download the `.jar` files using Maven build tools.

> Maven is a build tool that is widely used in Java application development. Its main feature is dependency management. You don't need to worry about dependencies of the JAR. It's automatically taken care of once you declare the parent dependency. You need to define a dependency using group, artifact ID, and version. All dependencies have to be declared in `pom.xml`, which is the heart of the Maven project.
>
> You can refer to `https://maven.apache.org` for more details.

You need to mention the following details in your `pom.xml` file to declare dependency of the Couchbase client in your Java project if you want to download the `.jar` files using Maven. The client library JARs will be downloaded in the local repository of your desktop and will automatically be included in the Java `CLASSPATH` variable of your project:

```
<dependencies>
    <dependency>
        <groupId>com.couchbase.client</groupId>
        <artifactId>java-client</artifactId>
        <version>2.1.3</version>
    </dependency>
</dependencies>
```

We will develop the Couchbase application using the Maven tools later in this chapter. Let's summarize what we have discussed till now. SDK can be used to store and retrieve documents from the Couchbase cluster. APIs also provide asynchronous methods so that applications don't need to wait for completion of operations, and Couchbase SDK will notify the application at the end of the operation.

Understanding the Couchbase API

Any database operation usually falls under one of the four categories of CRUD (Create, Read, Update, and Delete). What is CRUD really about? Whenever we develop an application that requires some information to be stored at the backend, before performing any activity we need to store the data, which is the primary role of any database. This is represented by C to signify creation of record in the database. Then, we fetch data for manipulating or displaying, which is represented by R to signify a read operation. Sometimes, we need to update or delete data after it is stored in the database, that is, U and D signify the update and delete operations, respectively. Most databases provide these basic operational features. Couchbase also provides these with different operation names.

CRUD operations using the Couchbase API

Let me introduce some operations and their different forms provided by Couchbase for performing CRUD operations. These are abstract methods. The actual implementation will be specific to the SDK, which we will be discussing later in the chapter. The Couchbase SDK provides a different implementation of these abstract methods; however the underlying concepts remains the same.

Create

We can store information in the Couchbase bucket using the create operations. Here, we will discuss operations that are provided to insert documents into the cluster from the client:

- `set (key, value)`: This operation stores a document in the Couchbase bucket with the key as the document ID, and the value is the data or the document that needs to be stored in the bucket. If the document ID is already present in the bucket, it will be replaced.

- `add (key, value)`: This operation is used to store or add a document to the bucket. It will raise an exception if the document ID is already present in the bucket. You can use this operation if you don't want any accidental update of an existing document ID.

Read

The read operations enable clients to fetch documents from Couchbase buckets. Here, we will discuss an operation that is provided to read documents from the cluster by the client:

- `get (key)`: This operation retrieves a document using the key that is the document ID of the document. It will retrieve null or give an exception if the particular documented ID doesn't exist in the bucket, depending on the client API.

Update

The update operations enable the client to update existing documents in Couchbase buckets. We will now discuss two kinds of operations used to update a document in the Couchbase cluster; they are:

- `replace (key, value)`: This operation will update the document whose document ID, represented by the key; matches the document ID of the document in the bucket. It will throw an exception when executed if the document ID is not present in the bucket. This is different from the `upsert` operation, which will insert a document if it is not present in the bucket, else `update`

- `cas (key, value, cas)`: This operation is called compare and swap. The main feature of this method is that it will verify the metadata's `cas` value of the document before performing a replace operation. It will be successfully executed only if the `cas` value of the document in the bucket matches that of the `cas` parameter supplied along with the operation. Otherwise, it will throw an exception. This method is important, as it helps to prevent updating a stale document. You will understand more about this when we discuss locking later in this chapter.

Delete

The operation used to delete a document from the Couchbase bucket is as follows:

- `delete (key)`: This operation deletes a document with the specified document ID parameter. It marks the document to be deleted. The document will be deleted when the compaction process is executed.

A description of key and value

key: This represents the document ID of the document that is stored. It is part of the metadata information about a document.

value: This represents the actual document that is stored in the bucket. The value can be a string or a serializable object.

These are a few common operations provided by the Couchbase cluster. Besides these, there are other operations, such as increasing counter value, prepending and appending a value of a document, and so on. We will discuss these in the next section, *Understanding Java SDK*.

In addition to the operations we discussed previously, there are also two operations that are very important and used frequently by application programmer. They are observe and flush. You might still remember that, while performing write operations, documents get stored in memory, and the client gets an acknowledgment without waiting for documents to get written to the disk. This might be an issue for a particular scenario where we want every document to be stored on the disk without any exceptions. Using the observe method, we can determine whether the document is stored on the disk or not.

Also, there is an option available, while configuring buckets, to enable flush or not. If you enable this option, the contents of this bucket can be removed entirely in one operation; this is the functionality of the flush operation. You need to be very careful when enabling this option in the production environment, since it can remove entire documents stored in the bucket, including the one on the disk. The ideal scenario for using this option is when you need to store documents temporarily, for example, in analytics, and need to flush all documents after some time.

There is an operation called touch that increases the lifetime of a particular document by the time defined in the operation. This operation will be useful when you want to increase the lifetime of a document after performing an operation. There are some operations that provide asynchronous method calls using callback methods, in which the client doesn't need to wait for completion of operations. Such operations will be executed in another thread.

You need to keep in mind that all operations require a key, which is the document ID. No operation can be performed without it. All of these APIs support atomicity for a document. There is no specific locking mechanism while performing any of these operations in the cluster.

Understanding Java SDK

We discussed the various APIs provided by the Couchbase SDK for connecting to the Couchbase server and performing operations on it. Let's now try to focus on the APIs specific to Java. We are going to explain Java SDK 2.1.3. If you are a seasoned software developer, you might have some ideas about what are required to perform operations on the database system. We need to know the hostname or the IP address of the servers that run the Couchbase database. Of course, you need the database name, which is the bucket in the Couchbase system, to connect to it before performing any operations:

```
Cluster cluster = CouchbaseCluster.create();
Bucket defaultBucket = cluster.openBucket();
```

The preceding statements create a Cluster object using a `CouchbaseCluster` factory class, which will be used to connect to the bucket. If you didn't specify any parameters to the `create()` method, then it will connect to the localhost; that is, Couchbase should be running on the server in which the client application will be running. If we didn't specify any parameters while opening the bucket, it means that we are using the default bucket.

If we want to specify the Couchbase node while opening a connection, we can specify it as a parameter of the `create` method. You can also provide multiple server nodes using the `create` method by separating each node with a comma. The `openBucket()` method also accepts the bucket name if you are going to connect to buckets other than the default one:

```
Cluster cluster =
CouchbaseCluster.create("172.168.27.1",172.168.15.2");
Bucket beerSampleBucket = cluster.openBucket("LearningCouchbase");
```

After you have performed all operations on the bucket, you can close a connection to the Couchbase cluster using the following method:

```
cluster.disconnect();
```

CRUD operations using the Java SDK

There are various overloaded methods provided for performing CRUD operations using the Java SDK. It's not possible to mention all the APIs here. However, you can refer to the documentation at `http://docs.couchbase.com/sdk-api/couchbase-java-client-2.1.3/`.

In this chapter, we will discuss only the main methods that will be required most of the time in any application development. Make sure that you familiarize yourself with these methods, which I am going to discuss thoroughly later.

Insert

Listed here are two insert method signatures that can be used to create or insert a document in Couchbase:

- D insert(D document)

  - **Description**: This will insert a document, represented by a document variable if the document ID is not present in the bucket. Otherwise, it will throw an exception, DocumentAlreadyExistsException. This method is part of the Bucket object.

  - **Input parameter**: This is an object of the Document type.

  - **Return value**: An object of the Document type.

A description of the document class

Document: This Java class represents a document that is stored in a Couchbase bucket

Method:

- content(): This returns the content of the document
- id(): This returns the document ID/key of the document, which is unique for each bucket

Note that D extends Document.

- D insert(D document, long timeout, TimeUnit timeUnit)

  - **Description**: This will insert a document if the document ID is not present in the bucket. Otherwise, it will throw an exception, DocumentAlreadyExistsException. This method is part of the Bucket object. When we specify the timeout parameter, the method will throw TimeoutException when the server cannot store documents in the managed cache of the cluster within the specified time.

  - **Input parameter**: This is an object of the Document type, time out or the operation and the unit for the timeout.

  - **Return value**: This is an object of the Document type.

Read

The following are three read method signatures that can be used to retrieve or get a document from Couchbase:

- `D get(D document)`
  - **Description**: This will retrieve a document from the bucket for the document ID specified by `D.id()`. This method is part of the `Bucket` object.
  - **Input parameter**: This is an object of the Document type.
  - **Return value**: This is an object of the Document type.

- `D get(D document, long timeout, TimeUnit timeUnit)`
  - **Description**: This will retrieve a document from the bucket for the document ID specified by `D.id()`. The timeout period is specified as well. This method is part of the `Bucket` object.
  - **Input parameter**: This is an object of the document type, time out for the operation, and the unit for the time out respectively.
  - **Return value**: This is an object of the Document type.

- `JsonDocument get(String id)`
  - **Description**: This will retrieve the document from the bucket for the document ID specified in the input parameter. This method is part of the `Bucket` object.
  - **Input parameter**: This is the document ID.
  - **Return value**: This is an object of the `JsonDocument` type. It implements `Document<JsonObject>`.

Update

Listed here are four update methods signature that can be used to update a document in Couchbase:

- `D replace(D document)`
  - **Description**: This will replace the document for the document ID, which is part of the parameter. If the document ID is not present in the bucket, it will throw a `DocumentDoesNotExistException` exception. This method is part of the `Bucket` object.
  - **Input parameter**: This is an object of the Document type.
  - **Return value**: This is an object of the Document type.

- D `replace(D document, long timeout, TimeUnit timeUnit)`
  - ○ **Description**: This will replace the document for the document ID, which is part of the parameter; if the document ID is already present in the bucket. This method is part of the `Bucket` object.
  - ○ **Input parameter**: This is an object of the Document type, the timeout period, and the unit of the timeout respectively.
  - ○ **Return value**: This is an object of the Document type.

Upsert

The `Upsert` method enables us to insert documents into the Couchbase cluster, if it's not already present in the bucket, else it will update it.

- D `upsert(D document)`
  - ○ **Description**: This will insert or update a document for the document ID specified in the input parameter. If the document is already present, it will update the document. Otherwise, it will insert the document. This method is part of the `Bucket` object.
  - ○ **Input parameter**: This is an object of the Document type.
  - ○ **Return value**: This is an object of the Document type.

- D `upsert(D document, long timeout, TimeUnit timeUnit)`
  - ○ **Description**: This will insert or update a document for the document ID specified in the input parameter with the time-out parameter. If the document is already there, it will be updated; otherwise, it will be inserted. This method is part of the `Bucket` object.
  - ○ **Input parameter**: This is an object of the Document type.
  - ○ **Return value**: This is an object of the Document type.

Delete

The following are two delete method signatures that can be used to delete a document from Couchbase:

- D `remove(D document)`
  - ○ **Description**: This will delete a document for the document ID specified in the input parameter. This method is part of the `Bucket` object.
  - ○ **Input parameter**: This is an object of the Document type.
  - ○ **Return value**: This is an object of the Document type.

- D remove(D document, long timeout, TimeUnit timeUnit)
  - ○ **Description**: This is an overloaded method, as you have seen, but with timeout parameters

Touch

Listed here are two touch methods signature that can be used to increase the time to live of a document:

- Boolean touch(D document)
  - ○ **Description**: This resets the expiration time of a document in the bucket for the document ID specified in the input parameter with the default value. This method is part of the Bucket object.
  - ○ **Input parameter**: This is an object of the Document type.
  - ○ **Return value**: This can be True or False. It signifies the success of the operation.
- Boolean touch(String id, int expiry)
  - ○ **Description**: This will increase the expiration time of a document in the bucket for the document ID specified in the input parameter. This method is part of the Bucket object.
  - ○ **Input parameter**: This is the document ID and the expiry time.
  - ○ **Return value**: This can be True or False. It signifies the success of the operation.

Implementation – a Maven project for CRUD operations using the Java SDK

We have discussed the internal mechanisms of Couchbase operations and the various APIs that allow you to connect to Couchbase and perform operations in great detail. I can understand how you feel now, overwhelmed with theory and concepts. Once we write some application code, you will have better clarity. So, hold on till you complete this section.

Now let's write an application using the Couchbase Java API, and you should be able to replicate this code in your production environment too. But hold on till I show you the full-fledged code that performs CRUD operations. Let's first have a brief overview of the application that we will be developing using Java SDK. At the end of this section, you will be able to execute a program that connects to the cluster and performs CRUD operations.

The application consists of the following classes:

- LearningCouchbaseView
- LearningCouchbaseBO
- LearningCouchbaseDAO
- Customer
- ConnectionUtil

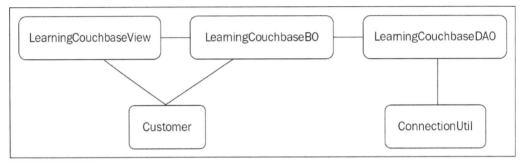

A class diagram depicting the dependencies of the classes

We are going to use the Eclipse IDE to create a Maven project for developing applications that connect to Couchbase and perform CRUD operations using various APIs discussed earlier. You can use any other IDE such as netbeans if you are already comfortable with it.

> **You can download the latest stable releases from these links**:
> - **Eclipse**: `http://www.eclipse.org/downloads/`
>   `packages/eclipse-ide-java-developers/lunasr2`
> - **Maven**: `http://www.carfab.com/apachesoftware/`
>   `maven/maven-3/3.3.3/binaries/apache-maven-`
>   `3.3.3-bin.tar.gz`

To create a Maven project perform the following steps:

1. Start eclipse and go to **File | New | Other | Maven | Maven Project**.
2. Create a Maven project with the following details:
   - `modelVersion: 4.0.0`
   - `groupId: com.ht`
   - `version: 0.0.1-SNAPSHOT`

3. The final `pom.xml` file, which is the configuration file of the Maven project should be as follows. We have declared dependencies of the Google `gson` `library` and `couchbase` client libraries in it. It will download all necessary JAR libraries required for this project:

```xml
<project xmlns="http://maven.apache.org/POM/4.0.0"
xmlns:xsi="http://www.w3.org/2001/XMLSchema-instance"
xsi:schemaLocation="http://maven.apache.org/POM/4.0.0
http://maven.apache.org/xsd/maven-4.0.0.xsd">
    <modelVersion>4.0.0</modelVersion>
    <groupId>com.ht</groupId>
    <version>0.0.1-SNAPSHOT</version>

    <dependencies>
      <dependency>
          <groupId>com.couchbase.client</groupId>
          <artifactId>java-client</artifactId>
          <version>2.1.3</version>
      </dependency>
      <dependency>
        <groupId>com.google.code.gson</groupId>
        <artifactId>gson</artifactId>
        <version>2.2.4</version>
      </dependency>

</dependencies>

  <artifactId>LearningCouchbase</artifactId>
</project>
```

4. Create the `LearningCouchbaseView` class. This will be the main class that will execute the CRUD operations. It will call all necessary underlying business object methods:

```java
package com.hp.view;

import java.util.ArrayList;
import java.util.List;

import com.ht.bo.LearningCouchbaseBO;
import com.ht.vo.Customer;

public class LearningCouchbaseView {

  public static void main(String[] args) {
```

```java
      LearningCouchbaseBO theBo;

      try {
        theBo = new LearningCouchbaseBO();
        // Create(theBo);
        // Read(theBo);
         Update(theBo);
        //Remove(theBo);
      } catch (Exception e) {
        // TODO Auto-generated catch block
        e.printStackTrace();
      }



    }

    static void Create(LearningCouchbaseBO theBo) {
      List<String> skills = new ArrayList<String>();
      skills.add("Spark");
      skills.add("Analytics");
      skills.add("Hadoop");
      Customer cust = new Customer();
      cust.setBook("Learning Spark");
      cust.setName("Henderson P");
      cust.setSkills(skills);
      theBo.createCustomerDocument(cust);
      System.out.println("Done");

    }

    static void Read(LearningCouchbaseBO theBo) {

      Customer myCust =
theBo.findCustomerDocument(theBo.docID);
      System.out.println(" Book Name: " + myCust.getBook());

    }

    static void Update(LearningCouchbaseBO theBo) {

      Customer myCust = theBo.findCustomerDocument(theBo.docID);
      myCust.getSkills().add("Predictive Models");
      theBo.updateCustomerDocument(theBo.docID, myCust);
```

```
      System.out.println(" Skills Count : " + myCust.getSkills().
   size());
      }

   static void Remove(LearningCouchbaseBO theBo) {
      System.out.println(" Documented Deleted : " +
   theBo.deleteCustomerDocument(theBo.docID));
      }
   }
```

5. Add another class, LearningCouchbaseBO. This will be the business object class that accepts requests from the main program and calls data access layer objects subsequently:

```
package com.ht.bo;

import com.ht.dao.LearningCouchbaseDAO;
import com.ht.vo.Customer;

public class LearningCouchbaseBO {

   LearningCouchbaseDAO theDao;
   String cbHost = "127.0.0.1";
   String bucketName = "LearningCouchbase";
   String password = "";
   final public String docID = "2008";

   public LearningCouchbaseBO() throws Exception {
      super();
      theDao = new LearningCouchbaseDAO(cbHost, bucketName,
   password);
      }

   public void createCustomerDocument(Customer cust) {
      theDao.createCustomerDocument(docID, cust);
      }

   public Customer findCustomerDocument(String docID) {
      Customer cust = theDao.findCustomerDocument(docID);
      return cust;

      }

   public Customer updateCustomerDocument(String docID,
   Customer cust) {
```

```
      Customer updatedCust =
theDao.updateCustomerDocument(docID, cust);
      return updatedCust;


   }

   public boolean deleteCustomerDocument(String docID){
       theDao.deleteCustomerDocument(docID);
     return true;


   }
}
```

6. The `LearningCouchbaseDAO` class performs the actual call to the Couchbase cluster. The definition of this class is shown in the following code. All APIs related to Couchbase should be confined to this class only:

```
package com.ht.dao;

import com.couchbase.client.java.Bucket;
import com.couchbase.client.java.document.JsonDocument;
import com.couchbase.client.java.document.json.JsonObject;
import com.google.gson.Gson;
import com.google.gson.GsonBuilder;
import com.ht.util.ConnectionUtil;
import com.ht.vo.Customer;

public class LearningCouchbaseDAO {

   final  Bucket theBucket;


   public LearningCouchbaseDAO(String cbHost,String
bucketName, String password) throws Exception {
      super();
      theBucket = ConnectionUtil.getTheBucket(cbHost,
bucketName, password);
   }


   public long createCustomerDocument(String docID,Customer
cust){

      Gson gson = new GsonBuilder().create();
      JsonObject content = JsonObject.fromJson(gson.toJson(cust));
```

```
JsonDocument doc = JsonDocument.create(docID,content);
JsonDocument insertDoc = theBucket.insert(doc);
return insertDoc.cas();

}


 public Customer updateCustomerDocument(String docID,Customer
cust){

Gson gson = new GsonBuilder().create();
JsonObject content = JsonObject.fromJson(gson.toJson(cust));
JsonDocument doc = JsonDocument.create(docID,content);
JsonDocument updateDoc = theBucket.replace(doc);
return gson.fromJson(updateDoc.content().toString(), Customer.
class);

}
public Customer findCustomerDocument(String docID){

Gson gson = new GsonBuilder().create();
JsonDocument fDoc = theBucket.get(docID);
Customer cust = gson.fromJson(fDoc.content().toString(),
Customer.class);
return cust;

}

public boolean deleteCustomerDocument(String docID){

theBucket.remove(docID);
return true;

}
}
```

7. The `ConnectionUtil` is a utility class that provides the code to connect to the Couchbase cluster. Add this class to the project and define it as follows:

```
package com.ht.util;

import com.couchbase.client.java.Bucket;
import com.couchbase.client.java.Cluster;
import com.couchbase.client.java.CouchbaseCluster;

public class ConnectionUtil {
```

```
      static final Cluster cluster = CouchbaseCluster.create();
      static public Bucket getTheBucket(String cbHost,String
   bucketName, String password) throws Exception {
         Bucket bucket = cluster.openBucket(bucketName, password);
         return bucket;

      }

      static void closeTheBucketConnection() throws Exception {
         cluster.disconnect();
      }
   }
```

8. The `Customer` class is the value object class that is used to pass information between various layers that resemble a business object:

```
package com.ht.vo;

import java.util.List;


public class Customer  {

  String name;
  String book;
  List<String> skills;
  public String getName() {
    return name;
  }
  public void setName(String name) {
    this.name = name;
  }
  public String getBook() {
    return book;
  }
  public void setBook(String book) {
    this.book = book;
  }
  public List<String> getSkills() {
    return skills;
  }
  public void setSkills(List<String> skills) {
    this.skills = skills;
  }

}
```

Now, you have the complete code for executing all the operations.

9. Run Maven compile goals.

10. You need to uncomment the following statement in the
    `LearningCouchbaseView` class before executing the program:

```
    Create(theBo);
// Read(theBo);
//Update(theBo);
//Remove(theBo);
```

11. Run `LearningCouchbaseView` as a Java application.

You can execute step 11 multiple times by commenting all the statements stated in the preceding code except one to perform CRUD operations one after another. You can also verify the document state using the Couchbase administrator web console after each operation.

Understanding locking

In any database system, whenever a client is trying to update a record, it acquires a lock in that record so that another client cannot update the same record. This is done to maintain consistency in RDBMS.

Sometimes, when we perform a bulk update, this locking of records escalates to locking a table, and all access is denied to that particular table. This has an adverse impact on the application's performance. A majority of the application performance issues that arise in the production environment happen due to locking of records or tables. There are various levels of locking in RDBMS depending on the application logic requirement. In my experience as a SQL DBA, I have often observed queries getting timed out while waiting to get locked on a particular record, which is already being locked by another query impacting the application's performance. I have spent a lot of time determining locks that a particular query has on a table to understand its impact on performance. It was really a nightmare!! This is the main bottleneck in most database systems, sometimes leading to deadlock too. Likewise, there is a mechanism for locking a document in Couchbase. However, it (luckily) doesn't escalate to the bucket level. This mechanism will surely bring a sigh of relief to you if you are a DBA for a large-scale application.

Before discussing the Couchbase locking mechanism, let's understand the types of locking. There are two types of locking, as explained here:

- **Pessimistic**: In this case, it is assumed that the chance of updating a document by an activity while an action is being performed by another activity is very high, so a lock is acquired on the document while performing an action on it by the first activity itself. This is provided by the GETL operation. In simple terms, get the lock while performing an activity.

- **Optimistic**: In this case, it is assumed that another activity won't update a document while an operation is being performed on it by an activity. However, we must ensure that the document is not updated while we are performing an operation by any other process or if we have a stale document. This is incorporated by the CAS operation. In simple terms, get the document without the lock, but verify, before updating, that it was not updated by another process in between.

Get with Lock (GETL)

We have understood the locking mechanism and discussed about its types. The pessimistic locking is implemented using the getAndLock() method as shown here:

```
public Customer getCustomerDocumentWithLock(String docID){

    Gson gson = new GsonBuilder().create();
    JsonDocument fDoc = theBucket.getAndLock(docID, 25);
    Customer cust = gson.fromJson(fDoc.content().toString(), Customer.
class);
    return cust;


}
```

The preceding function will lock the document for 25 seconds at the time of retrieval. The default value is 15 seconds if you don't specify it, and you can lock a document for a maximum period of 30 seconds only.

How do we unlock it? A document will get unlocked automatically after being locked by a client when any of the following three events occur:

- The document is updated by an operation with a matching CAS value

- The 30-second period or the locking time has passed

- The unlock() command is issued, as shown here:

```
boolean result = theBucket.unlock(fDoc);
```

CAS

We have already discussed optimistic locking in the previous section. If we need to use it, we need the CAS value while performing the CAS operation. How do we get this value?

The CAS value will be retrieved when you perform the `get` operation, and it gets populated in the CAS field of the return document:

```
Gson gson = new GsonBuilder().create();
JsonDocument fDoc = theBucket.get(docID);
Customer cust = gson.fromJson(fDoc.content().toString(),
Customer.class);
System.out.println(fDoc.cas());
// 1434538056506593803
```

The last line displays the returned CAS value. The value will be different when you execute it, since it's a number that is internally generated by Couchbase.

When your application updates a document using the `replace` command, the operation will throw a `CASMismatchException` exception if the CAS value does not match the one stored in the Couchbase document:

```
JsonDocument updateDoc = theBucket.replace(doc);
```

 If you don't want to use this CAS feature in your operation, you can change the CAS value in your document to 0. It will ignore the CAS value while performing the operation.

Understanding counters

There are times when we would like to have some counters defined to keep a track of documents. For example, if we want to track the sales of the book, *Learning Couchbase*, we can define a counter and increment it by 1 whenever someone buys the book. A counter can also be used to keep a track of users visiting the web page. It can be done as shown here:

```
theBucket.counter("NumberOfCopies", 1);
```

Initially, when the `NumberOfCopies` counter is not present in the bucket, it will be assigned a default value of 0. Here, the counter, `NumberOfCopies`, is increased by a value of 1.

async operations

Sometimes, applications perform operations on a database that doesn't need to wait until it is completed for further processing. Such operations will optimize resources in terms of CPU and disk I/O. Instead of holding the current thread and waiting for the response of that database queries, it proceeds further. Such asynchronous operations are allowed to use using Couchbase SDK. Let me show you a sample code and explain more about this:

```
AsyncBucket aBucket = theBucket.async();
  aBucket.get("2007").map(new Func1<JsonDocument, String>() {
                public String call(JsonDocument jsonDocument) {
                    jsonDocument.content().put("name"," Mr " +
jsonDocument.content().getString("name"));
                        return jsonDocument.content().getString("name");
                }
            }).subscribe(new Action1<String>() {

            public void call(String name) {
                System.out.println(" Async Call : " + name);
            }
        });

System.out.println(" Simple Get :" +
theBucket.get("2007").content().get("name"));
```

You will get the output as follows when you execute the program:

```
Async Call :  Mr Henry P
Simple Get :  Henry P
```

In this example, we load the document whose document ID is 2007 and prepend the salutation Mr to the name attribute. Now we can use the updated value, that is, Mr Henry P, further down in the application code for processing, that is, the document value is not appended in the bucket but in the application logic only. However, when we get the document again from the bucket with another operation, we get it as it is, without any salutation.

In order to use this asynchronous feature, you need to get AsyncBucket using the theBucket.async() method. Then you have to use the map() function to transform the document according to your business logic. Here, we add a salutation of Mr. Finally, it will be a callback to the call() method of the subscriber, which is registered using the subscribe() method.

This section is based on the Java Reactive programming APIs, Rx. You can learn more about it at http://reactivex.io/tutorials.html.

Connection management

By now, you have understood how to connect to the bucket and perform various operations using the Java SDK. We can conclude that there are two ways of connecting to the bucket:

- Synchronously:

```
Cluster cluster = CouchbaseCluster.create();
Bucket bucket = cluster.openBucket();
```

- Asynchronously:

```
AsyncBucket asyncBucket = bucket.async();
```

 It's best practice to create one instance of `CouchbaseCluster` per application.

Couchbase SDKs based on Java and .Net are designed to be thread-safe for each operation. There is a class called `CouchbaseEnvironment` that can be used to customize connection to the cluster.

How we create this environment is given in the following code:

```
CouchbaseEnvironment clusterEnv = DefaultCouchbaseEnvironment
        .builder()
        .computationPoolSize(5)
        .build();

    Cluster cluster = CouchbaseCluster.create(clusterEnv,
"ourserver.com");
```

You need to pass the `CouchbaseEnvironment` object to the cluster factory method while creating the cluster for the bucket. Don't forget to import the following package for this:

```
import com.couchbase.client.java.env.CouchbaseEnvironment;
import com.couchbase.client.java.env.DefaultCouchbaseEnvironment;
```

Let's review some of the main attributes that are provided by the
`CouchbaseEnvironment` class to customize the connection, as shown
in the following table:

Method	Remarks
`connectTimeout(long)`	This is the connection timeout for a connection to a bucket. The default value is 5,000 ms.
`reconnectDelay(Delay)`	When a connection is lost an attempt is made to reconnect with a delay. The default value is an exponential between 32 ms and 4,096 ms.
`keepAliveInterval(long)`	This is meant for sending the heartbeat to keep the information, from the client to the Couchbase node, alive. The default time is 30,000 ms.
`viewTimeout(long)`	This is the timeout for executing views. The default value is 75,000 ms.
`computationPoolSize(int)`	You can specify the number of threads in the connection pool. The default value is equal to the number of available processors.
`queryTimeout(long)`	This is the timeout for executing an N1QL query operation. The default value is 75,000 ms.
`queryPort(int)`	This is the port to connect for an N1QL operation. The default is 8093.

You can refer to the documentation for details on the other parameters at `http://docs.couchbase.com/sdk-api/couchbase-java-client-2.1.3/`. I don't want you to get overwhelmed by listing all the parameters available in the documentation. The aforementioned parameters are good enough for you to go ahead in your production environment.

Summary

We discussed how read, write, and delete operations work on the Couchbase server. Also, you understood various operations that are provided by the client SDK to connect and perform activities on the Couchbase cluster. We explored the concepts of the Java API. We also saw a full-fledged CRUD example. We touched upon the asynchronous operation provided by the Java SDK. Finally, we talked about customizing the connection properties.

In the next chapter, you will understand how to retrieve documents from Couchbase using views and how to write views using JavaScript. We will also discuss the concepts of MapReduce.

6
Retrieving Documents without Keys Using Views

So far, you have understood retrieving documents using the document ID only. However, most of the time, we would like to fetch documents using attributes other than the document ID. In this chapter, we will discuss how to retrieve documents using attributes of documents, when you don't know the document ID before hand. This functionality is provided by a mechanism called MapReduce programming, which is referred to as the term view in the Couchbase terminology. Before diving into views, let's discuss the concepts behind the working of MapReduce (MR) programming, which is the core of views. Hence, understanding it is essential in order to write a view efficiently. We will also discuss the life cycle of a view. Subsequently, we will discuss various features provided by views to filter documents, paginations, grouping, and ordering.

You will also learn how to perform SQL queries in the MapReduce format. You will then learn about various features of views, such as stale parameters, custom reduce, and so on. Then we will query these views from the Java program using Couchbase SDK APIs. By the end of this chapter, you will have a clear understanding of how to write efficient views to fetch documents from buckets and query them from a Java application.

An overview of MapReduce

What is MapReduce, or MR, all about? You might have heard a lot about this if you have been following technologies on big data for a while. Why do we need to understand it when we are trying to work on Couchbase's view? This is a way of programming, just like object-oriented programming. Since it's an abstract concept, you might find it hard to understand initially. Hence, I suggest you read it a couple of times until you understand it well. It's a concept, and you need to think in terms of MapReduce while developing applications using views to fetch documents. When we write a view in Couchbase to fetch documents from a bucket, we will be writing in the MapReduce format. Hence, understanding MapReduce is very crucial for writing views efficiently.

Nowadays, you might have read and heard a lot about big data, and whenever somebody talks about big data, people think of Hadoop and NoSQL databases. Big data is data that usually has characteristics of 3Vs. What is the purpose of these technologies? In earlier days, all the information was stored in RDBMS. However, the information growth rate has increased so tremendously that storing information in a single machine that has RDBMS is almost impossible. Although technologies and hardware, such as storage area network and network-attached storage, are available for storing a large amount of data, they are expensive to buy and maintain. Technologies such as Hadoop and NoSQL partition data efficiently across multiple nodes with minimal cost as compared to hardware solutions; enabling to store a large amount of data in a commodity's server.

The 3Vs are as follows:

Varieties: This means a varieties of data, such as text, blogs, pictures, videos, and so on

Volume: This is the large amount of data being generated

Velocity: This means that the rate at which data is being generated is very fast

So far, we have discussed Couchbase partition of information across the nodes within a cluster. Although we have taken care of storing large amounts of data across cluster nodes using data partition, the challenge is in processing the information store in the cluster. Let's take an example of a retail company, HT Enterprises, to understand how data can be processed using MapReduce. The company sells consumer goods such as clothes, shoes, jackets, and so on across the continents. It has 15,500 retail outlets all over the world. All transactions that occurred everyday in the POS, or point of sale, are centrally collected and stored in a Couchbase cluster. Data that gets generated everyday is about 1 TB and data for the last 2 years is maintained in the cluster, which is about 730 TB. The Couchbase cluster consists of 100 nodes, each having a storage capacity of 8 TB.

Now, the chairman of HT Enterprises has decided to reward the outlet that has performed the best in the last year in terms of sales. So, the marketing in-charge of HT enterprises sends an e-mail to the IT head of the company to provide details of the top three outlets with the highest total sales during the last year. How do you proceed if you are a database administrator who needs to provide this information?

There is no way a single machine can handle such a mammoth task of processing 730 TB data. MapReduce comes to the rescue. What MapReduce does is, as follows: your program goes to each of the nodes and performs processing on each node on the data that is stored in that particular node, the process executed in each node is called Map. Then, the output from each node is consolidated in a single process by the key, which is the reduce phase. Thus, it minimizes fetching of all documents at one node for overall aggregation; instead, it is aggregated in a single node after preprocessing each document, at each of the nodes where the document is stored. In MapReduce programming, there are two components, map and reduce, which work in tandem. Each of the records in the group or collection of input will be passed through the map function, and the output will be in the form of a key and value. The reduce method will accept a key and value, which is an array as a parameters. The reduce function will be called for each distinct key emitted from the map function as a key parameter along with the values array that has the same key. Grouping values of the same key in the form of an array or list and passing it as a parameter to a reduce task is usually taken care of by the framework, but here, it's Couchbase. You can find the pseudo-representation of the MapReduce function as follows:

```
map (K,V) --> K1, V1
reduce (K1,[V1,V2,...VN]) --> K,V
Note:- K --> Key and V --> Value.
 {
   "StoreId": "141526",
    "ItemId":"54378",
    "Quantity":"2",
    "Amount":"400",
     "Date":"05-05-2015"
 }
```

If we need to incorporate the earlier use case in the MapReduce format, the preceding sample document can be used to understand MapReduce programming. The preceding document represents a sales transaction of each retail outlets. Let me explain how MapReduce performs in our use case:

- **Map**: A Map program will be executed in each node of the cluster, and all the documents in that node will be passed as an input to that map process locally. Our logic of the map function will return the output as Store Id and Amount, as follows:

  ```
  return (141526,400) // (Store Id,Amount)
  ```

- **Reduce**: The Couchbase server ensures that the entire amount related to the same `Store Id` value will go to a single reduce process. So what will be the final output of our reduce? It will be the total sales amount of each store, as follows:

```
reduce (141526,[400,600,500,700])    // Input to the reduce
                   is the list of all values of the same key
   return (141526,2200) // sum of the sales amount
```

At the end, we have the total sales for each store, and finally, we can order the output by the total sales amount in descending order and get the top three stores for the rewards.

Let's understand the main advantages of MapReduce. In this process, all documents are passed through the map logic. It's the responsibility of the developer to write logic that needs to be performed on each document, such as filtering documents, depending on some attribute value such as *sale is greater than 1000*. Couchbase will ensure that the map program is pushed to each of the nodes in the cluster and execute it on all document's stores in the respective node, locally. This mechanism is opposite to the traditional ways in which data is pulled or stream to the application process. Whereas, in MapReduce, the program goes to the node where data is stored. Thus, the processing power of multiples nodes is fully utilized. Now that you have understood the concepts of MapReduce, let's move on to views.

Views

Whenever we want to extract fields from JSON documents without the document ID, we use views. If you want to find a document or fetch information about a document with attributes or fields of a document other than the document ID, a view is the way to do it. Views are written in the form of MapReduce, which we have discussed earlier, that is, it consists of the map and reduce phase. Couchbase implements MapReduce using the JavaScript language.

The following diagram shows you how various documents are passed through the **View Engine** to produce an index. The view engine ensures that all documents in the bucket are passed through the `map` method for processing and subsequently to the reduce function to create indexes:

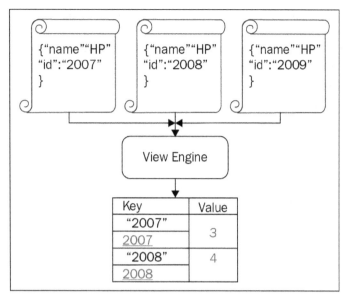

The View Engine

When we write views, the view engine defines materialized views for JSON documents and then queries across the dataset in the bucket. Couchbase provides a view processor to process entire documents with the map and reduce methods defined by the developer to create views. The views are maintained locally by each node for the documents stored in that particular node. Views are created for documents that are stored on the disk only. Hence, sometimes, there will be some documents missing in the views, which are mostly those documents that are in the RAM and that have not yet spilled on disks. The view's data is stored on the disk.

So why do we need to define views? We will be writing views to define primary and simple secondary indexes. Indexes help to fetch documents faster. Using views, we can perform aggregations (reduce phase) such as sum, min, and so on. The views are created only on those documents that are stored on disks, so what about documents that have not yet spilled on to the disks?

When a document gets spilled on to disks, they are eventually indexed. Thus, Couchbase ensures that whenever we execute views, documents are finally consistent with the views. Couchbase has provided a framework for MapReduce, and we only need to write map and reduce functions in the JavaScript language as shown in the following screenshot:

```
▼  VIEW CODE

Map

1    function (doc, meta) {
2      if(doc.skills) {
3        emit(meta.id, doc.skills.length);
4      }
5    }
```

Map views

The preceding screenshot shows a view. A view has predefined syntax. You can't change the method signature. Here, it follows the functional programming syntax. The preceding code shows a map function that accepts two parameters:

- doc: This represents the entire document
- meta: This represents the metadata of the document

Each map will return some objects in the form of a key and value pair. This is represented by the emit() method. The emit() method returns a key and a value, which can be a JSON document too. However, the value will usually be null. Since, we can retrieve a document using the document key, it's better to use the key to fetch the document instead of using the value field of the emit() method. If we emit a document as a value, it will consume more space. So, the recommended practice is not to emit any values.

You will mention the attributes of documents that need to be part of the indexes or the materialized view in the key of the emit() method. In our example, we have defined a map method that accepts two parameters: doc, which is the document, and meta, which is the meta data of the document.

In the first line, we verify that the document has a skills attribute. It is a best practice to verify the existence of an attribute before using it. Then, in the last line, we return the document ID as the key and the length of the skills attribute, as a value.

Types of views

There are two types of views, which are covered in the following sections.

Development

In the development view, an index is created on a subset of data. This will be used whenever we are developing a view, and we can make changes in it. Since it works on a subset of data, it will not take much time to build.

Production

Once we are okay with the development of a view, we can publish it as a production view, which will build indexes across the entire cluster nodes data. When we use production views for queries, queries will be scattered to all cluster nodes and the results are gathered from all nodes and returned to the client. You can't change a production view. Whenever you publish views to the production mode, it will take time as it creates views on all documents in the cluster. The duration depends on the number of records, and there will be a sudden spike in disk I/O and CPU usage. Let's suppose that after moving to production, you want to make some changes to the view. Then, you need to publish the production view to the development view and make changes on it. Later, you can again publish it to production.

A view's life cycle

A view has its own life cycle. You need to define, build, and query it, as shown in this diagram:

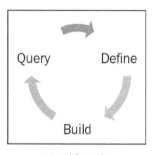

View life cycle

Initially, you will define the logic of the MapReduce and build it on each node for each document that is stored locally. In the build phase, we usually emit those attributes that need to be part of indexes. Views usually work on JSON documents only. If documents are not in the JSON format or the attributes that we emit in the map function are not part of the document, then the document is ignored during the generation of the view by the view engine. Finally, views are queried by clients to retrieve and find documents. After the completion of this cycle, you can still change the definition of MapReduce. For that, you need to bring the view to the development mode and modify it. Thus, you have the view cycle as shown in the preceding diagram while developing a view.

Before we go ahead and define views using the view editor, let me introduce the concept of bucket's design document. For manageability, all views are attached to a design document. So, whenever you want to write a view, you need to create one design document to attach the view into it. A design document can have multiple views. However, whenever any changes take place in one of the views' definitions in a single design document, all views that belong to that design document are rebuilt. This will increase the I/O and CPU usage across the Couchbase cluster. Hence, ensure that you group views in a design document that are not going to change its view's definition often.

The steps for creating views are as follows:

1. Create design documents on a bucket.
2. Create views within that design document.

The design document belongs to a data bucket, as shown in the following diagram:

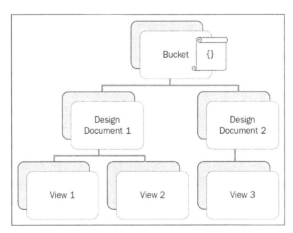

As you can see, each bucket can have multiple design documents, and each design document can have multiple views.

You also need to remember that views are created on documents that are stored on the disk only. Documents that are in the memory and are yet to be spilled over to the disk won't be part of the view build. This means that when the view engine processes the view definitions, it will only pass those documents that are on the disk to the map function. However, all documents will eventually be part of views when they get spilled onto the disk subsequently. Once a view is created on all documents in a bucket, subsequent build will be incremental. The documents in the bucket which are already persist on disks will not be built again for creating views. Even indexes can be replicated across nodes within the cluster to improve performance when the replicas are promoted to active, which happens when the active nodes fail.

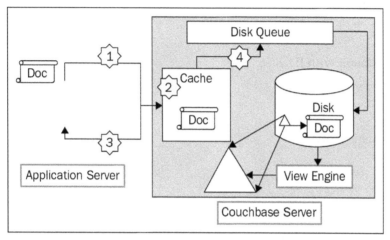

View creation flow

Once you define a view definition and build it, the Couchbase view engine generates a JSON structure on disk, which is a view of documents that are stored in the bucket. In this view, we can query and get a result set, which can further be allowed to iterate using APIs. It is not possible to perform query directly on the actual document that we store in the bucket. Views help us to find documents using certain attributes, which we store as a part of documents. Whenever documents are updated, views are finally updated once the documents get spilled onto the disk from the memory. There might be some latency when an updated document is spilled from the memory to the disk. You need to keep in mind that documents with expired timestamps might be part of views until compaction takes place and the view is updated accordingly. All views are updated eventually.

In order to understand views, let's create two documents with document IDs 2007 and 2008, as follows:

This is a document with ID 2007

```
{
  "name": "Henry P",
  "book": "Learning Couchbase",
  "skills": [
    "Couchbase",
    "Cassandra",
    "MongoDB"
  ]
}
```

This is a document with ID 2008

```
2008
{
  "skills": [
    "Apache Camel",
    "OSGI",
    "Map Reduce",
    "Fuse ESB"
  ],
  "name": "Henderson P",
  "book": "Learning Spark"
}
```

The views editor

Now that we discussed what a view is and its internal working, let's write a view. We will be using the views editor, which can be accessed using the web console. Open the web console, click on the **Views** tab, and then select the **LearningCouchbase** bucket, which you created earlier. You need to ensure that the development view is selected in the view console. Then click on **Create Development View**. This allows you to enter the design document and the view names. Click on **Save**, as shown in the following screenshot. The view details that need to be entered are as follows:

- **Design Document Name**: LCDD

 Couchbase appends _design/dev_ at the start.

- **View Name**: `findUsersWithSkills`

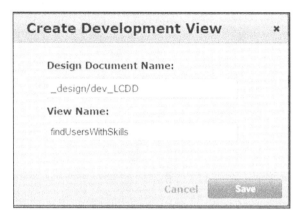

The view creation console

Couchbase will automatically prepend the design document name with `dev_` to signify that the design document belongs to the development view.

You will see the following screen after saving it. This is the view editor, where you are going to write MapReduce for a view. In the first row, you can find the name of the bucket, **LearningCouchbase**; the name of the design document, **dev_LCDD**; and the name of the view, **findUsersWithSkills**, as shown in the following screenshot:

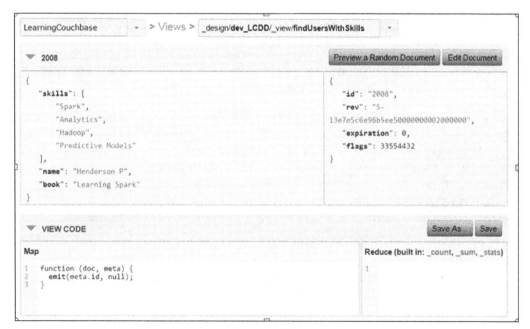

The views editor

The second row of the views editor, on the left-hand side, randomly displays a document from the bucket so that you can view it for reference while writing your map function. On the right-hand side, you will be able to view the metadata of that document.

In the last row, you can write the map and reduce functions. You can specify the map code on the left side, and on the right side, you can specify the reduce code.

Change **Map** as follows and save it:

```
function (doc, meta) {
   if(doc.skills) {
      emit(meta.id, null);
   }
}
```

The Map editor

The first line of the map is the signature of the map function; you can't change it. It accepts two variables: doc and meta. The doc variable represents the entire document in the bucket, and meta represents the metadata of the document. Inside the function, we filter only those documents that have the skills attribute. Then, we emit the document ID and the value as null.

Surprised that we are emitting null as value? This is not to consume much disk space. The best practice is to emit value as null and emit the attribute you want to search for in the key; here, in our case, document ID is the key. After getting the document ID, we can subsequently use the get function to derive the document from Couchbase. However, in various smart clients, such as Java API, smart SDK clients provide a mechanism to fetch the entire document using the document ID while you iterate the result set. This map function will be called for each document in the bucket.

Once the view is created for all documents in the bucket, the view engine only processes those documents that get created or updated afterwards. You can even incorporate logic and filtering of documents in the map function. The key and value of the emit method can be a single value, string, or compound value. The output of the view is sorted by key.

We will discuss the `reduce` function later in this chapter. After updating the `map` function, you can verify the result using the **Show Results** button, as shown in the following screenshot:

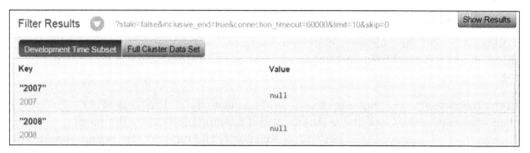

The Show Results pane

You can also access the result of the view using the following URL:

```
http://localhost:8092/LearningCouchbase/_design/dev_LCDD/_view/
findUsersWithSkills?stale=false&inclusive_end=true&connection_
timeout=60000&limit=10&skip=0.
```

```
{"total_rows":2,"rows":[
{"id":"2007","key":"2007","value":null},
{"id":"2008","key":"2008","value":null}
]
}
```

The view output

The view can also be invoked using the REST APIs. The output of our view is shown in the preceding screenshot, which is a JSON document. It displays the total number of records returned by the view, which can be accessed using the `total_rows` attribute. There is another attribute called `rows`, which is an array of value returned by the `map` function. Couchbase returns meta IDs along with a return value emitted by the `map` function. You can verify from the preceding screenshot, where `id` is 2007 which is part of the view result set, although it is not part of the `emit()` method.

Accessing a view using Java API

We have seen how to create a view using the views editor. Let's invoke it from application using the Java API.

You can use the existing Maven project that was created in the previous chapter. You need to add the following classes to that project. We will focus on methods that connect to Couchbase and use to execute our view, and use the view result set to display it.

In the following LearningCouchbaseViewDAO class, the data access layer class connects to the Couchbase cluster and it has one method by the name findAllUsersWithSkillset, in which we specify the name of the design document as, dev_LCDD, and the view that needs to be executed, findUsersWithSkills as a parameter to the from method of the ViewQuery class.

Then, we pass the ViewQuery object to the query method of the Bucket object. It returns a collection of ViewRow and this can be iterated through to fetch all documents returned by the view:

```java
package com.ht.dao.view;

import com.couchbase.client.java.Bucket;
import com.couchbase.client.java.view.ViewQuery;
import com.couchbase.client.java.view.ViewResult;
import com.ht.util.ConnectionUtil;

public class LearningCouchbaseViewDAO {

  final  Bucket theBucket;


   public LearningCouchbaseViewDAO(String cbHost,String bucketName,
String password) throws Exception {
     super();
     theBucket = ConnectionUtil.getTheBucket(cbHost, bucketName,
password);
   }

   public ViewResult findAllUsersWithSkillset() {

     ViewQuery query = ViewQuery.from("dev_LCDD",
"findUsersWithSkills");
     ViewResult result = theBucket.query(query);
```

```
      return result;
    }
```



```
}
```

In the `LearningCouchbaseViewBO` business object class, we convert `ViewRow` to the `Customer` object using the `GsonBuilder` library:

```
package com.ht.bo.view;

import java.util.ArrayList;
import java.util.List;

import com.couchbase.client.java.view.ViewRow;
import com.google.gson.Gson;
import com.google.gson.GsonBuilder;
import com.ht.dao.view.LearningCouchbaseViewDAO;
import com.ht.vo.Customer;

public class LearningCouchbaseViewBO {

  LearningCouchbaseViewDAO theDao;
  String cbHost = "127.0.0.1";
  String bucketName = "LearningCouchbase";
  String password = "";

  public LearningCouchbaseViewBO() throws Exception {
    super();
    theDao = new LearningCouchbaseViewDAO(cbHost, bucketName,
password);
  }
  public List<Customer> findUserDocumentWithSkills() {
    Iterable<ViewRow> result = theDao.findAllUsersWithSkillset();
    Gson gson = new GsonBuilder().create();
    ArrayList<Customer> custList =  new ArrayList<Customer>();
        for(ViewRow row : result) {
            Customer cust = gson.fromJson(row.document().content().
toString(),
Customer.class);
            custList.add(cust);
        }

    return custList;


  }
}
```

The `LearningCouchbaseView` class is the class that finally displays values that we have emitted from the `map` function of the view:

```java
package com.ht.view;
/**
 *
 * Written By : Henry Potsangbam
 * Dated : 6th July 2015
 * Description: Main Program for performing Views operation using
JAVA SDK
 *
 *
 */
import java.util.List;

import com.ht.bo.view.LearningCouchbaseViewBO;
import com.ht.vo.Customer;

public class LearningCouchbaseView {

  public static void main(String[] args) {
    LearningCouchbaseViewBO theBo;

    try {
      theBo = new LearningCouchbaseViewBO();
      ReadAllUsers(theBo);

    } catch (Exception e) {
      // TODO Auto-generated catch block
      e.printStackTrace();
    }
  }
  static void ReadAllUsers(LearningCouchbaseViewBO theBo) {

    List<Customer> myCustList = theBo.findUserDocumentWithSkills();
    for (Customer myCust : myCustList) {
      System.out.println(" Book Details: " + myCust.getBook() + "
" + myCust.getSkills());
    }


  }

  }
```

When you execute the preceding program, you will get the following details, which display the `skills` for all documents in the bucket returned by the view:

```
Book Details: Learning Couchbase   [Couchbase, Cassandra, MongoDB]
Book Details: Learning Spark   [Spark, Analytics, Hadoop,
Predictive Models]
```

Indexes

You have understood what a MapReduce program is and how it is used to create views in the Couchbase cluster. A view helps us to retrieve or search for a document by attributes of the document other than the document ID. In a database terminology, which is called an index, that enables to fetch documents using some look up mechanism, indexes help to search for a document in an efficient manner. As discussed earlier, MapReduce allows to create views/indexes on documents that is stored locally on each node. Index creation occurs in parallel in each node within the cluster. Finally, when clients query views, the results from all nodes are combined and provided to clients. Indexes and views are optimized for search and aggregations, which will be performed in the `reduce` function. The output of the `map` function is stored in a B-tree format, to enable fast retrieval. Whenever you want to fetch documents using attributes of documents, you can create views, which in turn will create indexes on the keys emitted by the `map` function. Then, you can use that key to filter documents. You can create multiple indexes in a bucket. However, you need to keep in mind that it can create overhead and will use extra disk storage.

There are parameters to enforce rebuilding of indexes/views while fetching documents using views by clients. Besides this, active and replica indexes are updated if there are at least 5,000 new changes for every three seconds of inactivity. This duration is configurable.

In short, all output keys of the `emit` function are stored as indexes to enable an efficient document search. Since we have created indexes on the document ID, the view or index that was created in the previous section is called primary index. We will be able to create various types of indexes subsequently in the following sections.

Understanding stale parameters

Whenever we change the definition of a view, the entire view is recreated. In order to minimize overhead, ensure that you verify the logic of the view at the development stage before moving it to production, since it works on sample documents of the bucket. Subsequent changes to documents are taken care of by performing incremental MapReduce on the changed documents only. There is a mechanism for updating views conditionally when the client executes a view query by specifying the `stale` parameter. The indexes information stored on the disk consist of a combination of both key and value information defined within your view. There are three values of the `stale` parameter:

- `update_after`: This is the default value if nothing is specified. When a client executes a view with a stale value as `update_after`, the result will be served with index documents that is on the disk, and subsequently Couchbase will start performing an incremental view rebuild for those documents that are not part of index.

Stale value with `update_after` will always get a fast response, since it doesn't need to recreate the view before serving the response. You can specify the stale value as part of the query string, as shown here:

```
http://localhost:8092/LearningCouchbase/_design/
dev_LCDD/_view/ findUsersWithSkills?stale=updat
e_after&inclusive_end=false&reduce=false&connecti
on_timeout=60000&limit=10&skip=0
```

- `ok`: When a client invokes views with stale = ok, it will be served immediately, without updating the index. It will use the view information available at the time of query invocation.

This will provide a fast response, since it will use the existing index only.

You can specify the `stale = ok` as part of the query string, as shown here:

```
http://localhost:8092/LearningCouchbase/_
design/dev_LCDD/_view/ findUsersWithSkills?sta
le=ok&inclusive_end=false&reduce=false&connect
ion_timeout=60000&limit=10&skip=0
```

- `false`: When clients use the `false` value in the `stale` parameter, it instructs Couchbase that it wants views to be rebuilt before serving the request, just in case there is any change or addition of documents in the bucket. However, keep in mind that this will delay the serve request, since Couchbase needs to rebuild the index before responding to the request. You can use this option if you require up-to-date information all the time when documents are being fetched from the bucket using views. For example, if you want to find the maximum amount of sales on a particular day from the documents that contain sales by each store. In this scenario, we need to account for all documents created in the bucket, including the one that is in the RAM but yet to spill onto the disk.

>
> Here, we can specify `stale=false`, as shown in the following query string:
>
> ```
> http://localhost:8092/LearningCouchbase/_design/
> dev_LCDD/_view/findUsersWithHighSkills?stale=f
> alse&inclusive_end=false&reduce=false&connecti
> on_timeout=60000&limit=10&skip=0
> ```

Built-in reduce functions

Often, we want to perform summarized/aggregate operations on data, such as count or grouping of documents by some attributes and using it to report or get statistics about some documents. This kind of grouping of data or documents takes place in the `reduce` function of the view. For example, we want to find the total number of users in our `LearningCouchbase` bucket, the total number of skill sets by the user, and so on. The `reduce()` function will reduce an array of values emitted by the corresponding `map()` function. Couchbase ensures that the `reduce` function is applied to each record of the input parameter, and the returned value is the result of the view. The output of the reduction is stored along with the view information. There are three in-built `reduce` functions provided by Couchbase out-of-the-box.

count

The `count` function is used to count the number of documents emitted by the `map` function. You need to set the `reduce` parameter equal to `true` to use the `reduce` function. You can specify the group level parameter to group the key in the `reduce` function.

The following screenshot shows the `reduce` method with the `count` function:

count - reduce

When you want to group by all the keys together, you can specify the parameter, `group_level = 0`, as shown here. It will count all the documents:

```
Group Level = 0


?stale=ok&group_level=0&inclusive_end=true&connection_timeout=6000
0&limit=10&skip=0&reduce=true
```

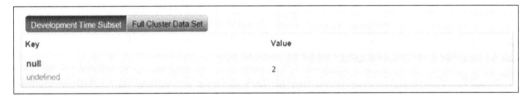

group_level = 0

When you want to determine the count of the document for each key, you can specify `group_level = 1`, as shown here. It will count all the documents grouped by the key. Here, there are two keys, `2007` and `2008`, whose counts are shown separately:

```
Group Level = 1
?stale=ok&group_level=1&inclusive_end=true&connection_timeout=6000
0&limit=10&skip=0&reduce=true
```

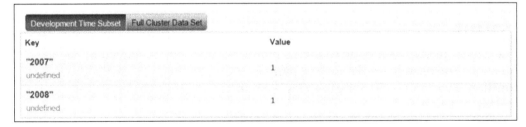

group_level = 1

sum

The sum function sums the values emitted by the map function for each group of rows by key.

```
VIEW CODE                                              Save As    Save

Map                                          Reduce (built in: _count, _sum, _stats)

1   function (doc, meta) {                   1    _sum
2     if(doc.skills) {
3       emit(meta.id, doc.skills.length);
4     }
5   }
```

sum - reduce

The preceding screenshot shows the view that define sum aggregation in reduce function. The following screenshot shows the result set with sum reduce function:

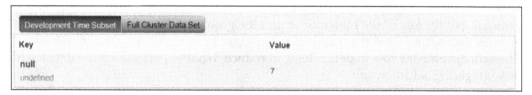

Key	Value
null	7
undefined	

sum reduce result

stats

The stats function produces statistical calculations for values emitted by the map function call for each group of rows by key. It generates statistics such as sum, count, minimum (min), maximum (max), and square of sum (sumsqr) of the input rows.

```
VIEW CODE                                              Save As    Save

Map                                          Reduce (built in: _count, _sum, _stats)

1   function (doc, meta) {                   1    _stats
2     if(doc.skills) {
3       emit(meta.id, doc.skills.length);
4     }
5   }
```

stats reduce

The output of views with stats reduce is shown as follows:

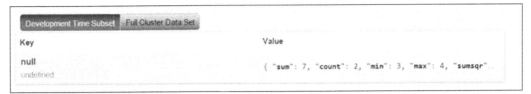

stats reduce - results

Custom reduce functions

Why do we need custom reduce functions? Sometimes, the built-in reduce function doesn't meet our requirements, although it will suffice most of the time.

Custom reduce functions allow you to create your own reduce function. In such a reduce function, output of map function goes to the corresponding reduce function group as per the key of the map output and the group level parameter. Couchbase ensures that output from the map will be grouped by key and supplied to reduce. Then it's developer's role to define logic in reduce, what to perform on the data such as aggregating, addition etc.

To handle the incremental MapReduce functionality (that is, updating an existing view), each function must also be able to handle and consume it's own output. In an incremental situation, the function must handle both new records and previously computed reductions.

The input to `reduce` function can be not only raw data from the map phase but also output of a previous reduce phase. This is called re-reduce, and can be identified by the third argument of `reduce()` function. When re-reduce argument is `false`, both the key and value arguments are arrays, the value argument array matches the corresponding element with that of array of key. For example the `key[1]` is the key of `value[1]`. The map to reduce function execution is shown as follows:

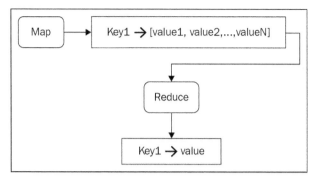

MapReduce execution in a view

Before we create another view with `reduce` function, let's create two more documents with document IDs, 2009 and 2010:

The document ID 2009:

```
{
  "skills": [
    "Enterprise Integration",
    "IoT",
    "Android",
    "Pehtaho"
  ],
  "name": "Tiraj P",
  "book": "Learning IoT"
}
```

The document ID 2010:

```
{
  "skills": [
    "OSGI",
    "TOGAF",
    "Mobile Analytics",
    "Cassandra"
  ],
  "name": "Henry P",
  "book": "Learning OSGI"
}
```

Let's create another view with the following details:

- View name: `findUsersWithHighSkills`

- Design document: `dev_LCDD`

- The `map` function:

```
function (doc, meta) {
   if(doc.skills) {
     emit(doc.name,doc.skills.length);
   }
}
```

- The `reduce` function:

```
function(key, values, rereduce)
{

 var result = {name:"", total: 0};
 for(var i=0; i < values.length; i++){
  if(rereduce){
    result.total =result.total + values[i].total;
    result.name = key[0];
  } else {
    result.total = sum(values);
    result.name = key[0];
   }
  }
  return   result;
}
```

In `reduce` function, `key` is the unique key derived from emitted key of `map()` function and `group_level` parameter. The values argument is an array of all values that match a particular emitted key. In `reduce` function, when the `rereduce` parameter is true, it indicates that the `reduce` function is again called as part of re-reduce. This value will be assigned by Couchbase; the developer doesn't have any control over it. However, they need to write logic for handling `rereduce` separately when `rereduce` value is set to `true` by the Couchbase. The `reduce` function should be able to consume the function's own output.

After defining the `reduce` function, you can click on the arrow beside **Filter Results** to fill in the filtering parameters, as shown here:

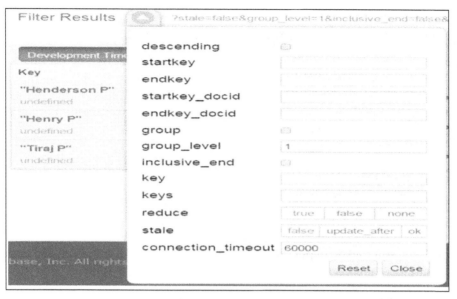

The Filter Result screen

You can select **reduce** as **true**; when you want to enable `reduce` function for a views and the **stale** parameter can also be selected, using this console. You can also specify descending order of the result set by selecting the **descending** checkbox, which is the first option in the preceding screenshot. The **descending** option is applicable on the key emitted by the `map` function; by default, it's in ascending order. You need to enter `1` in the **group_level** textbox. We will discuss other parameters in the next section. Next, click on the **Show Results** button to verify result set returned by the view. You can see the result as follows:

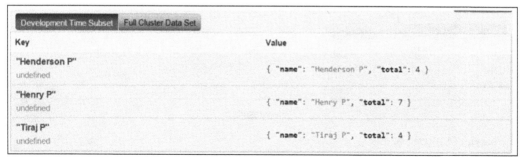

View result set

The result set is grouped by the key. In our case, the result set is grouped by the **name** attribute, and we have the total of the different skills possessed by a user.

Filtering and transforming data

We have written views in the form of map and reduce functions. A view creates indexes and stores them on disk for all documents with the output of map function, along with reduce function's output. Couchbase provides a filtering mechanism for documents generated by views. We can also perform some transformation on data using; the **group level**, which is discussed subsequently.

Using keys

We can specify key values to filter documents while querying views, like this:

```
key="2008"
```

We can also specify a key explicitly to get only that particular key's details. Here, we will get only the view record that pertains to the 2008 key, as follows:

The following screenshot shows the interface to key in the, key to filter indexes:

Key interface

When you execute the view with the preceding key filter, you will only see records that pertain to the particular key, as shown here:

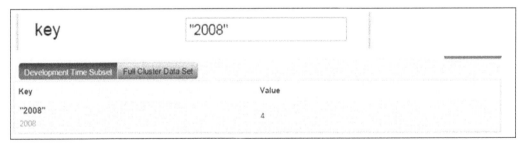

View result

```
keys=["2007","2008"]
```

We can explicitly specify a list of keys to get only those particular keys' details. In this case, we will get only the view data that pertains to the ["2007","2008"] key's array.

You can specify the keys' ranges in the interface, as shown here:

keys	["2007","2008"]

The key ranges interface

When you execute the view with the ranges, the result set is shown as follows:

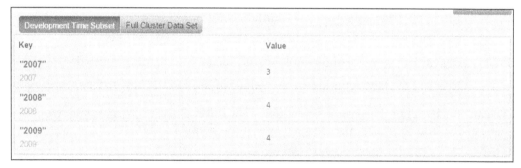

The view result set

```
startkey="2007"&endkey="2009"
```

We can also specify a range of keys. The preceding line will show all the records starting with 2007 and ending with the 2009 key, as shown in the following screenshot:

Development Time Subset	Full Cluster Data Set	
Key		Value
"2007"		
2007		3
"2008"		
2008		4
"2009"		
2009		4

The View result set

Pagination

We can incorporate pagination into the result set of a view using the skip and limit parameters:

```
?skip=2&limit=3
```

This will skip the first two documents and fetch the next three documents.

Internally, the view will be executed, two records will be iterated, and the next three records will be returned.

Grouping

When the key is a compound key, we can specify the `group_level` parameter to be applied to the query output. By enabling the group and specifying the group level, the output is grouped according to the key array:

```
?group=true&group_level=1&key=["2008","2009"]
```

Whenever we want to group by key and generate unique values, we can specify the array index, beginning with 1. Group level 0 groups the entire dataset without any further subgrouping. Group level 1 groups the result set by the unique value of the first key element of the compound key.

Ordering

The content of the key is used by the view to sort the result set automatically. Some particular format is used to sort by the following orders:

- Null: It represent null value
- False: It represents Boolean false value.
- True: It represents Boolean true value.
- Numbers: This key represents numeric value.
- Text: This key is case sensitive and ordered as lowercase first
- Arrays: This key depends on the values of each element in the order
- Objects: This key depends on the values of keys in the key order

We can specify all of these parameters using the **Filter Result** screen, which we have seen earlier, and these can also be specified in the Java API.

Mapping with SQL to MapReduce

We can perform most SQL operations in views also. We only need to change the way we visualize data extraction from the database using SQL and think in terms of the map and reduce functions. Here, we will see how to incorporate SQL queries into the MapReduce format.

Select and where conditions

Any fields or attributes selection for a document from a bucket can be performed by adding it to the emitted key or the value of the map function, which can be used for selection of attributes in the result set or for performing aggregation in the reduce function. The key generated by the map() function determines the ability of the view to query the bucket. Whenever you want to select documents based on some attributes of a document, you need to mention all those attributes that need to be part of the conditions as part of the key emitted by the map function.

Wherever conditions enable filtering of result set is required, it can be in cooperated using parameters such as key, keys, or startkey-endkey combinations to indicate data that needs to be selected. You need to ensure that the documents' attributes are part of the key emitted by map function if you want to use it in conditional parameters:

```
?key="2008"
```

```
http://localhost:8092/LearningCouchbase/_design/dev_LCDD/_view/findUs
ersWithSkills?key=%222008%22
```

```
{"total_rows":4,"rows":[
{"id":"2008","key":"2008","value":4}
]
}
```

The preceding example can be interpreted in SQL as follows:

```
Select * from Learningcouchbase where key = '2008'
```

Order by

The order by clause allows us to order documents while fetching using views. It can be performed using the order parameter. You can specify the ascending or descending value for the order parameter. Ordering is controlled by the value of the key.

Group by

The group by clause allows us to provide a summary of data for a group of records using a sum, count, or total operation in the reduce function.

Understanding geospatial views

A Couchbase bucket can also store two-dimensional spatial records specifying longitude and latitude. If you want to create a view for spatial records, it can be done using a geospatial view. This is introduced as an experimental feature and can be used in the development environment only. You can refer to the documentation for any update on this.

The following document represents the location of the city, Mumbai, in the bucket:

```
{
"location" : 18.9750, 72.8258],
"city" : "Mumbai"
}
```

You can create geospatial view as follows:

```
function(doc, meta)
{
  if (doc.loc)
  {
     emit( {  type: "Point", coordinates: doc. location, },
doc.location);
  }
}
```

The key in the spatial view index can be any valid GeoJSON geometry value.

View writing guidance

There are some design considerations that you need to keep in mind while writing views. These guidelines will help you maintain views efficiently.

Couchbase updates all views that are in the same design document at the same time. This will result in increased index building time and high disk I/O operations. You can design by grouping frequently used views into a separate design document. However, you can improve the overall performance of views by grouping views into smaller numbers of design documents.

You should avoid too much computing in one view; it will affect performance of the view. If your view is complex, it will consume CPU resources while performing rebuilds of indexes. Whenever you require a reduce function, ensure that you use built-in reduce functions, which are optimized, instead of using custom reduce functions, which can hamper performance. You must also make sure that you verify the existence of the attribute before using it in the view logic, since the schema is dynamic in nature. You should refrain from emitting a document as a value from the map function of the view. The detailed document can always be fetched using the document ID whenever the client requires it using the GET API. When you emit too many values, it will increase the disk size consumption along with the disk I/O. You can also replicate indexes across the nodes within a cluster. When you enable this, it will increase the disk size along with the CPU usage and storage I/O.

You should also ensure that instead of emitting the entire document, you can emit meta ID in a map function. Whenever you require a filter on a document, you can use views to filter it in the map function itself. By default, Couchbase builds four active and two replica design documents in parallel. You can configure it by changing the `maxParallelIndexers` and `maxParallelReplicaIndexers` parameters from the Couchbase CLI.

Summary

We discussed MapReduce and how to write it in Couchbase using JavaScript and using the view editor of the web admin console. You also learned about the life cycle of a view. Then we discussed the stale parameter, how to write a custom reduce, and finally, the fact that all of these views are accessible from Java applications.

In the next chapters, we will discuss N1QL, which is like the structured query language of RDBMS.

7
Understanding SQL-Like Queries – N1QL

In the previous chapter, you learned how to fetch documents using the MapReduce functionalities of views. Therein, you need to create a view before querying for any documents when not using a document ID. Couchbase has developed an efficient way of retrieving documents using a SQL-like syntax, called N1QL. N1QL is simpler and easier to understand. The syntax is more or less like that of SQL, so developers who are from RDBMS's SQL background will find themselves very much at home.

This method makes it easier to retrieve information from Couchbase. The main difference between SQL and N1QL (pronounced as Nickel) is that N1QL provides a way to query the JSON based document-oriented database, Couchbase. N1QL offers a **data definition language (DDL)**, a **data manipulation language (DML)**, and queries to extract information in Couchbase.

In this chapter, we will see how to set up N1QL to fetch data from a bucket using SQL-like syntax, and then discuss the various syntaxes used to manipulate a document in the bucket. After understanding its features, you will learn more about APIs in order to connect to N1QL to fetch and insert data.

The N1QL overview

So far, you have learned how to fetch documents in two ways: using document ID and views. If you are reading this book sequentially from the first chapter, you will agree with me. Otherwise, I recommend that you go through *Chapter 6, Retrieving Documents without Keys Using Views*, in order to understand this chapter better.

The third way of retrieving documents is by using N1QL. Personally, I feel that it is a great move by Couchbase to provide SQL-like syntax, since most engineers and IT professionals are quite familiar with SQL, which is usually part of their formal education. It brings confidence in them and also provides ease of using Couchbase in their applications. Moreover, it provides most database operational activities related to development.

N1QL can be used to:

- Store documents, that is, the INSERT command
- Fetch documents, that is, the SELECT command

Prior to the advent of N1QL, developers need to perform key-based operations, which were quite complex when it came to retrieving information using views and custom reduce. With the previously available options, developers needed to know the key before performing any operation on documents, which would not be the case all the time. Before N1QL features were incorporated in Couchbase, you could not perform ad hoc queries on documents in a bucket until you created views on it. Moreover, sometimes we need to perform joins or searches in the bucket, which is not possible using the document ID and views. All of these drawbacks are addressed in N1QL. I will rather considers N1QL features as an evolution in the Couchbase history.

 At present, the latest N1QL **Developer Preview 3** (**DP3**) is out there; however, it should not be used in production. My recommendation is to use N1QL for all development purposes once the official release is out.

Installing and configuring N1QL

One of the most interesting features of N1QL is providing the option of joins, wherein you can retrieve information from multiple documents with the JOIN clause. We will see this in more detail subsequently in this chapter. Before taking a deep dive, let's first see how to install and configure N1QL. At the time of writing this book, N1QL is a separate component that needs to be installed separately, besides Couchbase. You can download the .exe file from the Couchbase website. Some options might not work in the DP3. At present, Couchbase has released Couchbase Server 4.0 BETA, which incorporated N1QL along with the Couchbase installation itself. It supports DDL and DML operations. However, up to DP3, the features provided are more on SELECT clause, that is, fetching documents from the bucket.

You can download DP3 from `https://s3.amazonaws.com/query-dp3/couchbase-query_dev_preview3_x86_win.zip`.

After you download DP3, extract it to a folder of your choice (in my case, it is in `D:\MyExperiment\Couchbase`), go to the folder, and execute the following command to connect to the Couchbase cluster:

```
cbq-engine -couchbase http://localhost:8091/
```

```
D:\MyExperiment\Couchbase>cbq-engine -couchbase http://localhost:8091/
10:50:44.220788 Info line disabled false
10:50:44.283795 tuqtng started...
10:50:44.283795 version: v0.7.2
10:50:44.284795 site: http://localhost:8091/
```

The CBQ engine

The preceding screenshot displays the command to start a CBQ (Couchbase query) engine, which will be listening for N1QL queries on the 8093 port, to execute it in the Couchbase cluster.

The `couchbase` parameter in the preceding screenshot represents any node of the Couchbase cluster. Alternatively, you can run `start_tutorial.bat` (windows environment) for a hands-on tutorials provided by Couchbase for learning. After you start the batch file, you can open `http://localhost:8093/tutorial` in your browser.

If you want to use a command-line interactive query tool, you need to ensure that, earlier, cbq engine command prompt was not closed in order to connect using CLI:

```
cbq -engine=http://localhost:8093/
```

```
D:\MyExperiment\Couchbase>cbq -engine=http://localhost:8093/
cbq>
```

CBQ CLI

The preceding screenshot displays the CBQ CLI, for executing N1QL queries.

You can execute queries in this CLI.

The N1QL query engine

The core of N1QL preview is the query engine that listens for query requests on port 8093. In order to execute N1QL queries, you can use the cbq command-line shell, which comes with the developer preview, or HTTP requests to the <cbq-host>:8093/query endpoint, where <cbq-host> is, of course, the machine on which you start the query engine.

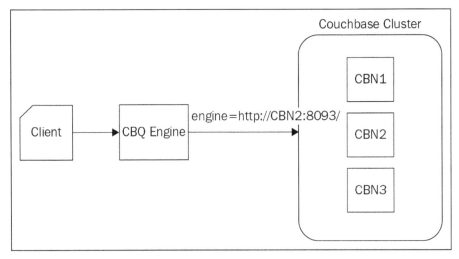

N1QL connectivity

As you can see in the preceding diagram, you need to pass the CBQ engine parameter to connect to the Couchbase cluster. The parameter can be the address of any of the nodes of the cluster. Here, we have connected to the Couchbase node 2. You can unzip N1QL P3 in any of the existing nodes or on a separate server.

Operation types

With the release of DP4, N1QL is a full-fledged SQL-like language meant to fetch and perform various operations on a JSON based document stored in the bucket. Since we are working on N1QL DP3, we will only discuss the features provided by it, as follows:

Category	Description
Select	This provides features to extract the desired attributes from documents present in the bucket
Filter	You can filter documents according to the conditions of your application logic
Aggregate	You can perform aggregation by grouping attributes specified in the aggregate clause
Having	You can filter documents on the aggregate value after applying aggregation functions
Order	You can order resultset documents
Skip	You can perform skipping of records while fetching documents
Join	This can join multiple documents

You will be executing all these types of queries from the Couchbase Query Engine CLI or from client APIs. We will be showing you all this queries' examples using CLI, for your understanding.

You can execute the following queries on your Couchbase cluster:

```
cbq -engine http://<cbq-host>:8093/
```

You need to create a primary index when you execute query for the first time. Let's create the primary index with the following command:

```
CREATE PRIMARY INDEX ON LearningCouchbase USING GSI
```

```
cbq> CREATE PRIMARY INDEX ON LearningCouchbase USING GSI
{
    "resultset": [
    ],
    "info": [
        {
            "caller": "http_response:160",
            "code": 100,
            "key": "total_rows",
            "message": "0"
        },
        {
            "caller": "http_response:162",
            "code": 101,
            "key": "total_elapsed_time",
            "message": "7.5337533s"
        }
    ]
}
cbq>
```

The primary index command

After that, you can execute this query:

```
SELECT * FROM LearningCouchbase
```

```
cbq> SELECT * FROM LearningCouchbase
{
    "resultset": [
        {
            "book": "Learning Couchbase",
            "name": "Henry P",
            "skills": [
                "Couchbase",
                "Cassandra",
                "MongoDB"
            ]
        },
        {
            "email_id": "hendersonp@ht.com",
            "name": "Henderson P",
            "password": "#!2007.CP:",
            "user_id": "hendersonp"
        },
        {
            "book": "Learning Spark",
            "name": "Henderson P",
            "skills": [
                "Apache Camel",
                "OSGI",
                "Map Reduce",
                "Fuse ESB"
            ]
        },
        {
            "book": "Learning IoT",
            "name": "Tiraj P",
            "skills": [
                "Enterprise Integration",
                "IoT",
                "Android",
                "Pehtaho"
            ]
        },
```

The from command

This selects all documents stored in LearningCouchbase bucket. Here, we fetched all documents stored in the LearningCouchbase bucket. The output of the query as shown in the preceding screenshot is in the JSON document format only. All the documents returned by the N1QL query will be in an array format which attribute, is represented by resultset.

You will understand the N1QL syntax in detail in the next section.

Understanding N1QL syntax

Most N1QL queries will be in the following format:

```
SELECT [DISTINCT] <expression>
FROM <data source>
WHERE <expression>
```

```
GROUP BY <expression>
ORDER BY <expression>
LIMIT <number>
OFFSET <number>
```

The preceding statement is very generic. It tells you the comprehensive options provided by N1QL in one statement. Let me break it down into parts so that it can be understood easily.

I will be explaining these N1QL query syntax based on documents stored in the bucket, LearningCouchbase, which we created earlier. If you remember correctly, we have already entered some documents in the LearningCouchbase bucket as well. We will execute the N1QL queries only on those documents.

If we want to fetch all the users' documents in the LearningCouchbase bucket, but want to display only some information or attributes, that is, the name and the book attribute of the documents, it can be done as follows:

```
SELECT name,book
FROM LearningCouchbase
```

Select Query

A generic SELECT statement is in the form of SELECT [DISTINCT] <expression> FROM <data source>, where expression is a literal value or can specify documents or its properties, and <data source> can be the name of the bucket or the path to the nested document along with the bucket name.

Now, as we can observe in the `resultset` of the last command, there is a repetition of usernames. If we want to find a unique user name in the bucket, how do we do this? We use the `DISTINCT` expression:

```
SELECT DISTINCT name
FROM LearningCouchbase
```

```
cbq> SELECT DISTINCT name FROM LearningCouchbase
{
    "resultset": [
        {
            "name": "Henry P"
        },
        {
            "name": "Henderson P"
        },
        {
            "name": "Tiraj P"
        },
        {}
    ],
    "info": [
```

Select with distinct feature

Then we wish to extract a document related to `LearningCouchbase` only:

```
SELECT *
FROM LearningCouchbase
WHERE book = 'Learning Couchbase'
```

```
cbq> SELECT * FROM LearningCouchbase where book = 'Learning Couchbase'
{
    "resultset": [
        {
            "book": "Learning Couchbase",
            "name": "Henry P",
            "skills": [
                "Couchbase",
                "Cassandra",
                "MongoDB"
            ]
        }
    ],
    "info": [
        {
            "caller": "http_response:160",
            "code": 100,
            "key": "total_rows",
            "message": "1"
        },
        {
            "caller": "http_response:162",
            "code": 101,
            "key": "total_elapsed_time",
            "message": "66ms"
        }
    ]
}
```

Select with where conditions

Besides the `resultset`, the query also returns some information about its execution. You can get the total number of rows returned by the query represents by the `total_rows` attribute under `info`, and the total execution time is specified by `total_elapsed_time`.

Let's try to find out how many skills each of the users has in their profiles. This will be obtained using the GROUP BY clause. Here, we will specify the username in the GROUP_BY clause along with the ORDER BY clause to display the user in the ascending or descending order by the skill set number:

```
SELECT [DISTINCT] <expression>FROM <data source>WHERE
<expression>GROUP BY <expression>ORDER BY <expression>
```

What do you do if you want to fetch only two records? You specify the LIMIT clause:

```
SELECT name,book
FROM LearningCouchbase
LIMIT 2
```

Select with limit

The preceding screenshot displays the `resultset` of the N1QL query with the LIMIT clause executed in the `LearningCouchbase` bucket.

Finally, suppose you want to skip some records and fetch the next two records. So, you have to specify an offset for it:

```
SELECT DISTINCT username,book
FROM LearningCouchbase
LIMIT 2
OFFSET 2
```

```
cbq>
cbq> SELECT name, book FROM LearningCouchbase LIMIT 2 OFFSET 2
{
    "resultset": [
        {
            "book": "Learning Spark",
            "name": "Henderson P"
        },
        {
            "book": "Learning IoT",
            "name": "Tiraj P"
        }
    ],
```

Select query with offset

Join

The most prominent feature provided by N1QL is the joining of documents, which is not possible in views. When you use the JOIN clause without specifying any quantifier, it will perform an inner join, which means that it will select only those documents from the left side of the join that have a matching key with that on the right side.

You now need to create a document in the LearningCouchbase bucket with the following details, using the Couchbase web admin console for the JOIN clause demonstration:

```
Document ID :CITY_001
{
  "city": "Mumbai",
  "userList": [
    "2008",
    "2009"
  ]
}
SELECT UD.name, CN.city
FROM LearningCouchbase AS CN JOIN LearningCouchbase UD KEYS ARRAY
user FOR user in CN.userList END
```

```
cbq> select UD.name, CN.city from LearningCouchbase as CN JOIN LearningCouchba>
<
    "resultset": [
        <
            "city": "Mumbai",
            "name": "Henderson P"
        >,
        <
            "city": "Mumbai",
            "name": "Tiraj P"
        >
    ],
```

N1QL with join

Cross-bucket joins

Another prominent feature of N1QL is that it supports cross-bucket joins. When might you need this? Suppose you have two buckets in your application. In one of them, you can store your master data, and in the other bucket, you can store your transactional documents. With this bucket join, you can fetch a document with details from another bucket, which was not possible earlier:

```
SELECT lc.name, bs.website

FROM LearningCouchbase AS lc

JOIN beer-sample AS bs

KEY lc.name
```

Query conditions and expressions

There are a lot of conditional expressions and operators that are built-in keywords in N1QL. Some of the important ones are listed here. You can refer to the documentation for the comprehensive list. Here is a list of operators:

Operator	Description	Operator	Description
=,>,<,!=,>=	This means equal to, greater than, less than, not equal to, and so on.	COUNT(expr)	This returns the number of items in a resultset.
AVG(expr)	This calculates the average of the attribute specified in the expression clause. The attribute should be a numeric value.	MIN(expr)	This returns the least of all values in a resultset.

Operator	Description	Operator	Description
CASE | WHEN | THEN | ELSE | END	This returns the values depending on the conditions.	ARRAY_AGG(expr)	This evaluate the expression for each member of the group and returns an array containing these values.
IS MISSING	This determines whether the field is missing in the document.	IS NOT NULL	This verifies an empty value of a field.

Sorting and grouping

You can order the resultset of a query using the ORDER BY expression:

```
SELECT count(*) AScount,name

FROM LearningCouchbase

GROUP BY name

ORDER BY name desc
```

Order By and Group By clause

In the preceding example, we extract the name attribute of all documents with the number of occurrences of the same name in the bucket. You can get the resultset by specifying the count and grouping by keywords. As shown in the preceding example, there is one user by the name Tiraj P, and another named Henderson P, who has two counts. We use count(*) to determine the occurrence of the record, which is grouped by the name attribute of documents.

We can use the HAVING clause to filter data derived from an expression after executing the query, as shown in this code:

```
SELECTcount(*) AScount,name

FROM LearningCouchbase

GROUP BY name

HAVING name Is valued AND count(*) > 1
```

```
cbq> select count(*) as count,name from LearningCouchbase group By name Having n
cbq> (on LearningCouchbase group By name Having name Is valued AND count(*) > 1
{
    "resultset": [
        {
            "count": 2,
            "name": "Henry P"
        },
        {
            "count": 2,
            "name": "Henderson P"
        }
    ],
```

Having clause

In this example, we fetch all the documents for which the minimum occurrence of a particular username is greater than 1.

Indexing properties

Querying an unindexed property causes the server to scan the entire bucket and check that property on every document. You can create indexes with the following syntax:

```
CREATE INDEX Index_name

ON LearningCouchbase(name)
```

Here, Index_name is the name of the index you want to create, LearningCouchbase is the name of the bucket, and name is the attribute of documents in which you want to create the index.

 One thing you need to remember is that you cannot execute any N1QL query until you create a primary index with the query shown next.

```
CREATE PRIMARY INDEX ON LearningCouchbase
```

Views

When you create indexes on a bucket; internally, Couchbase creates views on your behalf. As shown in the preceding screenshot, you can find views in the view editor after you create indexes.

Explaining a query

Sometimes, we like to know how queries will be executed in the Couchbase cluster. It helps us to tune it while in the development phase. You just need to append the EXPLAIN keyword before the query. It will return a JSON document that explains the execution plan, as shown in the following:

```
EXPLAIN SELECT * FROM LearningCouchbase
```

```
"resultset": [
    {
        "input": {
            "as": "LearningCouchbase",
            "bucket": "LearningCouchbase",
            "ids": null,
            "input": {
                "as": "",
                "bucket": "LearningCouchbase",
                "cover": false,
                "index": "#primary",
                "pool": "default",
                "ranges": null,
                "type": "scan"
            },
            "pool": "default",
            "projection": null,
            "type": "fetch"
        },
        "result": [
            {
                "as": "",
                "expr": {
                    "path": "LearningCouchbase",
                    "type": "property"
                },
                "star": true
            }
        ],
        "type": "projector"
    }
]
```

Explain execution

This is the sample `resultset` returned by the `EXPLAIN` query. It provides the query plan and some information of it without an actual execution. You can determine the bucket used in the N1QL query specified by the bucket attribute, which is `LearningCouchbase` in our example. This query will use the primary index as specified by the `index` attribute in the `resultset`, whose value is `#primary`. The `resultset.input.type=fetch` value means that the document is fetched via the document keys.

Using the N1QL API

Let's understand the Java APIs to use N1QL queries in our Java application. In order to demonstrate it, let's create another Maven project with the following details:

`ModelVersion: 4.0.0`

`GroupId: com.ht`

`ArtifactId: LearningCouchbaseN1QL`

You need to ensure that the following dependency is included in your `pom.xml` project:

```
<dependency>
<groupId>com.couchbase.client</groupId>
<artifactId>java-client</artifactId>
<version>2.0.0</version>
</dependency>
```

You also need to ensure that the version you use for this module is 2.0.0. At the time of writing this book, this is the only version compatible with the N1QL Developer Preview, which we have used in this book:

```
package com.ht.cql.view;


import com.couchbase.client.java.Bucket;
import com.couchbase.client.java.Cluster;
import com.couchbase.client.java.CouchbaseCluster;
import com.couchbase.client.java.query.QueryResult;
import com.couchbase.client.java.query.QueryRow;


/**
 *
 * Written By : Henry Potsangbam
 * Dated : 6th July 2015
```

```
 * Description: Main Program for performing Views operation using
JAVA SDK
 *
 *
 */


public class LearningCouchbaseCQLView {

  public static void main(String[] args) {
    boCQL();
  }

  static void boCQL() {
    System.setProperty("com.couchbase.queryEnabled", "true");
    Cluster cluster = CouchbaseCluster.create("localhost");

    Bucket bucket = cluster.openBucket("LearningCouchbase");

    QueryResult result = bucket.query("SELECT * FROM
LearningCouchbase where book Is valued");
      for(QueryRow row : result.allRows()) {
        System.out.println(" Book Details: " +
row.value().getString("name") + " " +  row.value().getString("book")
+ "   " +  row.value().getArray("skills"));
      }
  }


  }
```

We have declared one method, `boCQL()`, which connects and executes the N1QL query. We need to enable the N1QL execution features in our application using the system property, which can be set using the `System.setProperty("com.couchbase.queryEnabled", "true");` statement. Then, we connect to the `LearningCouchbase` bucket. Finally, we use the bucket object to execute the N1QL query. It will return the `QueryResult` object. We can then loop through the `QueryResult` object using its API method, `allRows()`, which returns an iterator.

You can execute the program and get the following output if you follow the same steps that were explained in the preceding section:

```
Book Details: Henry P Learning Couchbase  ["Couchbase","Cassandra","MongoDB"]
Book Details: Henderson P Learning Spark  ["Apache Camel","OSGI","Map Reduce","Fuse ESB"]
Book Details: Tiraj P Learning IoT  ["Enterprise Integration","IoT","Android","Pehtaho"]
Book Details: Henry P Learning OSGI  ["OSGI","TOGAF","Mobile Analytics","Cassandra"]
```

Congratulations! You have learned how to execute N1QL queries from a Java application.

Summary

In this chapter, we discussed N1QL. You understood its architecture, its various operations, and the syntax provided by it. We also executed some queries on the Couchbase cluster using the CLI. At the end, we showed how to connect to the CBQ engine and execute N1QL queries using Java APIs.

In the next chapter, we will provide an overview of ElasticSearch, integrate it with Couchbase, and provide a text search mechanism using it.

8

Full Text Search
Using ElasticSearch

In the earlier chapters, we discussed various ways to fetch documents from buckets. If you have gone through the book from the beginning, you might recall this. Let me repeat what has been covered in the last few chapters. We discussed the retrieval of documents using the document ID, views (using MapReduce programming in JavaScript), and N1QL (Couchbase query language).

You need to read the previous chapters to understand all of these in detail. But you might wonder why you need all of these? There are three ways to retrieve data. More precisely, you could call them an evolution or better ways of fetching documents, depending on the use case.

In this chapter, we will see how to integrate ElasticSearch with Couchbase so that we can perform full text searches. In the first section, we will take an overview of ElasticSearch, and then we will learn how to integrate ElasticSearch with the Couchbase cluster. After that, we will execute some queries on ElasticSearch. By the end of this chapter, you will learned how to use ElasticSearch in tandem with Couchbase.

Understanding content-driven applications

What is a content-driven application? Nowadays, most applications are driven by content only. For instance, e-commerce applications have a lot of contents in terms of catalogs, items descriptions, feedback, and so on. I am pretty sure that you must have browsed through at least one e-commerce website to buy something or the other. Let's say you are looking for a book on Couchbase, so you go to www. packtpub.com to search a book on this. You are at the homepage. Then what do you do? You will look for the search box, right? Luckily, you found it in the homepage in the middle of the page. Then, enter Couchbase in the search box. This box then displays the number of titles with the word Couchbase in it. Out of these options, Learning Couchbase is an option that you need to click on, as shown here:

An e-commerce site

It will display some details of the book. You can read the following details:

- **Book Details**
- **Table of Contents**
- **About This Book**
- **Who This Book Is For**
- **What You Will Learn**
- **Description**
- **Authors**

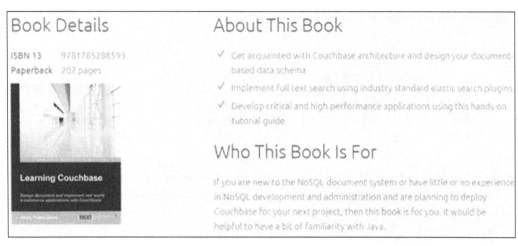

Book Details

ISBN 13   9781785288593
Paperback   202 pages

Learning Couchbase

Design document and implement real world
e-commerce applications with Couchbase

About This Book

✓ Get acquainted with Couchbase architecture and design your document-based data schema

✓ Implement full text search using industry standard elastic search plugins

✓ Develop critical and high performance applications using this hands-on tutorial guide

Who This Book Is For

If you are new to the NoSQL document system or have little or no experience in NoSQL development and administration and are planning to deploy Couchbase for your next project, then this book is for you. It would be helpful to have a bit of familiarity with Java.

An E-commerce site – product description

In some websites, you can provide reviews too. All of these are part of the contents. We usually go through reviews and descriptions before deciding to buy the book. All of these descriptions don't have a fixed schema, and Couchbase supports a schemaless storage of information in the form of a JSON document. Let's consider the following scenario: you are an area business manager of this particular e-commerce portal and you say, *We need to incorporate ratings for our books*; we can include this feature easily if we are using any document base system for storing information without changing any schemas. All of these flexibilities are provided by Couchbase too.

Suppose we have decided to incorporate all of these features such as descriptions, comments, reviews, and so on, and store all of the relevant contents of a book. Then, we need to provide a mechanism to search book documents by text in descriptions or comments, and so on. This can be made possible by full text search features only. We will cover this in more detail in the next section, and see how to implement it in Couchbase using ElasticSearch.

Full text search overview

Full text search enables searching of documents by text. It's applicable to a wide range of applications, such as e-business or even analytics (for example, performing sentimental analytics).

Let's add a description in our existing document, as follows:

```
{
    "book": "Learning Couchbase",
"description": "If you are new to the NoSQL document system or have
little or no experience in NoSQL development and administration and
are planning to deploy Couchbase for your next project, then this book
is for you. It would be helpful to have a bit of familiarity with
Java."
}
```

If we want to search for the term "NoSQL" in any document, we will be using the full text search across the full JSON body. Couchbase provides these features by integrating with ElasticSearch.

So what is this ElasticSearch?

ElasticSearch (ES) is a framework or tool that performs querying or searching of text in a JSON document and returns the documents that matched the search text, along with some statistical analysis of text with respect to the document. Technically, it behaves like a database that stores all of document's details in an index format so that it can be searched in a faster way. It supports clustering and scaling out, if required. ElasticSearch depends on the Lucene technology, which is its heart. It provides a lot of flexibility to search documents using the Java API. It also provides a wrapper around Lucene to use it with ease. ElasticSearch provides all its features in a REST API/JSON format.

ElasticSearch is a huge topic; we will try to explore it in brief here. We will discuss its main features and the terminologies that are required to understand how to integrate with the Couchbase cluster. You can refer to the ElasticSearch website, `https://www.elastic.co/`, for more details.

The following are the features of ElasticSearch:

- **Full text search**: ElasticSearch provides powerful full text search capabilities based on Lucene. These are easy to use.
- **Document-oriented**: ElasticSearch stores indexed data in a JSON-based document format and provides a RESTful API.
- **Schemaless**: No fixed schema is required to get started.
- **Analytics**: ElasticSearch provides real-time analytics capabilities with high availability.

I have mentioned just a few capabilities of ElasticSearch; you can find a comprehensive list of features on the ElasticSearch website.

Before configuring ES and using it, let's cover some terminologies you need to understand for proper usage of the ES query. A few important ES terminologies are listed here:

- **Document:** The basic unit that gets stored in ES for indexing is called a document. It's just like a record; for example, user information is a document. It's stored in a schemaless JSON format. Each document contains a set of attributes or fields, and they can be indexed for searching.

- **Index**: This is a logical namespace for grouping information or documents that have related information. It might contain documents of different types, such as user data, order details, and so on. An index has a unique name and is used while performing indexing and searching.

- **Type**: This is a subcategory inside an index. An index can have multiple types. In our `LearningCouchbase` example, we can have an index by the name `LearningCouchbase` and multiple types, say `User`, `Book details`, and so on, where `User` and `Book details` are different document entries in the bucket.

Configuration and query

In this section, we will configure ElasticSearch and integrate it with Couchbase.

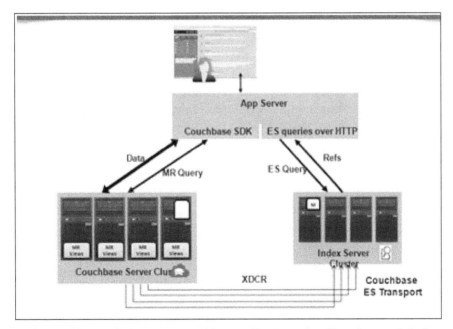

The Couchbase and ES integration architecture (Courtesy - Couchbase Documentation)

Let me briefly explain the architecture and usage pattern of ElasticSearch with the Couchbase cluster. Couchbase can replicate documents to ElasticSearch using XDCR, which will be discussed in detail in the next chapter. ElasticSearch will perform indexing on documents replicated from the Couchbase cluster by each attribute, and the developer will execute the search query in ES and use the resultset returned by ES to get the actual document from the Couchbase cluster, as shown in the preceding diagram. Why are we not storing the actual document in ES and fetching it from ES itself? In order to answer this query, you need to remember that ES is good for searching text and Couchbase is fast at data retrieval, since all documents are, by default, stored in the memory. Here, we are trying to use the best features of the two technologies. One is the search feature and the other is data retrieval using the `get()` method.

We need to perform the following steps to integrate ES with the Couchbase cluster:

1. You need to have the Couchbase cluster in place.
2. You need to install the ElasticSearch cluster.
3. Installation of head, a basic web UI tool, to interact with ES.
4. Installation of the ElasticSearch Couchbase Transport plugin.
5. Restart the ElasticSearch cluster after completing the above steps.
6. Create an ElasticSearch index for your documents.
7. Define XDCR between Couchbase and ElasticSearch.

We have already completed the first step in the first chapter. If you skipped that, ensure that you perform this step by going to that chapter. Let's proceed to install the ElasticSearch cluster. ES can be a single-node cluster. In our case, we will configure a single-node cluster only. You can start with a single cluster node and, if the performance deteriorates with more access demands by the application, you can scale out by installing more nodes. We are not discussing scalabilities here; you can refer to the ES documentation for that.

You can download `elasticsearch-1.5.2.zip` from `https://www.elastic.co/`
`downloads` or any latest version. Unzip it into a folder and you will find various
folders inside it, as follows:

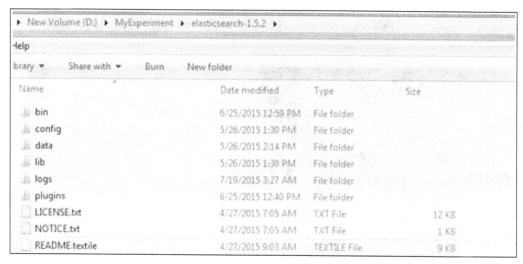

The ElasticSearch installation folder

You can verify the ElasticSearch installation; for this, you need to browse to the `bin`
installation folder and execute the following command:

```
cd ElasticSearch-1.5.2/bin

ElasticSearch  -server -XX:-UseSuperWord
```

```
D:\MyExperiment\elasticsearch-1.5.2\bin>elasticsearch.bat -server -XX:-UseSuperW
ord
[2015-06-23 16:55:57,647][WARN ][bootstrap               ] Workaround flag -XX:
-UseSuperWord for bug https://bugs.openjdk.java.net/browse/JDK-8024830 found.
This will result in degraded performance!
Upgrading is preferred, see http://www.elastic.co/guide/en/elasticsearch/referen
ce/current/_installation.html for current recommendations.
[2015-06-23 16:55:57,912][INFO ][node                    ] [Danielle Moonstar]
version[1.5.2], pid[7512], build[62ff986/2015-04-27T09:21:06Z]
[2015-06-23 16:55:57,912][INFO ][node                    ] [Danielle Moonstar]
```

The ElasticSearch startup

You can shut down the ElasticSearch cluster now till we configure it to integrate with the Couchbase cluster. Let's install ElasticSearch head, which is a web UI tool that provides a user interface for ES:

```
cd ElasticSearch-1.5.2/bin
plugin -install  mobz/ElasticSearch-head –urlfile:ElasticSearch-head-
master.zip
```

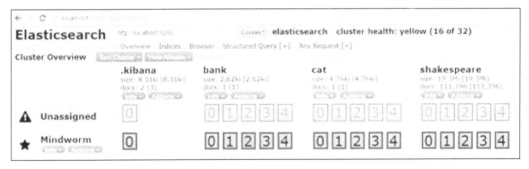

ES head installation

You need to ensure that you provide the complete path to the file location of `ElasticSearch-head-master.zip`. It can be download from the ElasticSearch website.

After this, you can start ElasticSearch and browse the head UI, as follows:

```
http://localhost:9200/_plugin/head/
```

ElasticSearch head

The UI might be a bit different from version to version, but it has more or less the same look and feel.

Now let's install the Couchbase plugin that will transport documents from Couchbase to ES. The installation is as simple as the Head UI plugin we installed just now.

You need to open a command window, browse to the ES installation `bin` folder, and execute the following command. You also need to ensure that the proper path is provided to the `transport-couchbase-{version}` `.zip` file:

```
plugin -install transport-Couchbase -url file:D:\ElasticSearch-
transport-Couchbase-2.0.0.zip -verbose
```

```
D:\MyExperiment\elasticsearch-1.5.2\bin>
D:\MyExperiment\elasticsearch-1.5.2\bin>
D:\MyExperiment\elasticsearch-1.5.2\bin>plugin -install transport-couchbase -url
   file:D:\elasticsearch-transport-couchbase-2.0.0.zip -verbose
-> Installing transport-couchbase...
Trying file:D:/elasticsearch-transport-couchbase-2.0.0.zip...
Downloading ........................DONE
Installed transport-couchbase into D:\MyExperiment\elasticsearch-1.5.2\plugins\t
ransport-couchbase
```

The Couchbase ES plugin

Before you use the transport plugin to replicate data from Couchbase to ES, you need to set the username and password for the credentials to connect to ES in the configuration file. For this, you need to open `{Installation folder}/conf/ElasticSearch.yml` and append the following after the last line:

- `couchbase.password`: `password`

- `couchbase.username`: `Administrator`

After you are done installing these two plugins, the head and transport components of the ES, you can start ElasticSearch:

`bin/ElasticSearch`

Now we have the Couchbase plugin for ElasticSearch and the ElasticSearch engine installed and running. Let's create index templates in the ES cluster to store documents replicated from the Couchbase cluster. We can replicate documents to ES from Couchbase only after this setup.

We are going to issue some commands on ES using `curl`, so you need to download curl and add it in the `PATH` variable. After that, we can execute the `REST` command to create a template for replicating the Couchbase document to ES index:

```
curl -XPUT http://localhost:9200/_template/Couchbase -d
@plugins/transport-Couchbase/Couchbase_template.json
```

```
D:\MyExperiment\elasticsearch-1.5.2>curl -XPUT http://localhost:9200/_template/c
ouchbase -d @plugins/transport-couchbase/couchbase_template.json
{"acknowledged":true}
D:\MyExperiment\elasticsearch-1.5.2>
```

ES mapping

Finally, for each Couchbase bucket we want to search using the ES query, we'll need to create a corresponding index in ElasticSearch to store document in it:

```
curl -XPUT http://localhost:9200/learningCouchbase
```

```
D:\MyExperiment\elasticsearch-1.5.2>curl -XPUT http://localhost:9200/learningcou
chbase
{"acknowledged":true}
D:\MyExperiment\elasticsearch-1.5.2>
```

Index creation

You can verify the index we just created, `learningcouchbase`, using the web UI, `http://localhost:9200/_plugin/head/`.

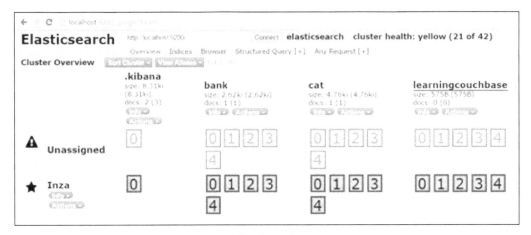

ES Head overview

You need to stop and start ElasticSearch for the configuration changes to take effect.

Now the final step is to configure XDCR to replicate documents to the ES cluster. What is this XDCR? It is cross-datacenter replication between Couchbase and any other supported cluster. We will discuss it in detail in the next chapter. As of now, remember that XDCR helps to replicate documents from Couchbase to ES for indexes and provides full text search capabilities.

In order to configure XDCR, you need to log on to the web Admin console and click on the **XDCR** tab. Under this tab, you can configure and start data replication between a source and a destination cluster. In this case, our source cluster is Couchbase and the destination is ElasticSearch.

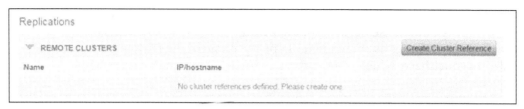

The XDCR console

Click on **Create Cluster Reference**. A panel appears, and you can specify information about our ElasticSearch cluster in it. In this, you need to specify the ElasticSearch cluster information in which the Couchbase server will replicate documents from the data bucket.

Enter a **Cluster Name**, **IP/hostname**, **Username**, and **Password** for your ES cluster, as shown in the following screenshot. Then click on **Save**.

You need to use the password that was specified in `ElasticSearch.yml` in the earlier section (it is `password`).

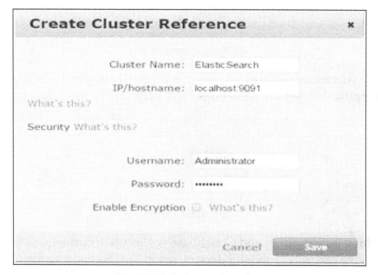

The XDCR cluster configuration

Finally, to initiate replication, click on the **Create Replication** button. Select the **LearningCouchbase** bucket and the **ElasticSearch** remote cluster from the drop-down boxes as shown here. Type the name of the remote bucket — **learningcouchbase**, which is the index in ES — as shown in this screenshot:

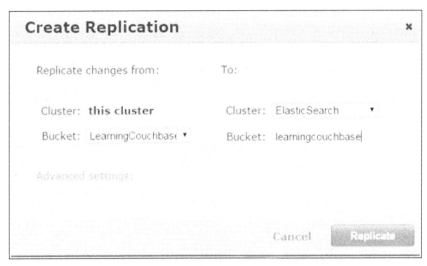

XDCR replication mapping

Then, click on **Advanced** settings and use the protocol version 1. Once you click on the **Create Replication** button, Couchbase will begin replicating documents to ES.

The XDCR status

Now, everything is configured and Couchbase replicates documents to ES. The system is ready when we can start searching documents in the ES cluster using ES query.

Let's search for one of my favorite books by opening `http://localhost:9200/`
`learningCouchbase/_search?q=Couchbase&pretty=true` in the browser.

```
{
  "took" : 11,
  "timed_out" : false,
  "_shards" : {
    "total" : 5,
    "successful" : 5,
    "failed" : 0
  },
  "hits" : {
    "total" : 2,
    "max_score" : 2.9908342,
    "hits" : [ {
      "_index" : "learningcouchbase",
      "_type" : "couchbaseDocument",
      "_id" : "2007",
      "_score" : 2.9908342,
      "_source":{"meta":{"id":"2007","rev":"2-13de13bcd891ef8700000000000000000","flags":0,"expiration":0}}
    }, {
      "_index" : "learningcouchbase",
      "_type" : "couchbaseDocument",
      "_id" : "2015051522",
      "_score" : 1.0574195,
      "_source":{"meta":{"id":"2015051527","rev":"5-13e64a342619000f00000000000000000","flags":0,"expiration":0}}
    } ]
  }
}
```

The ES query output

With the preceding URL, we search for the `Couchbase` keyword in ElasticSearch.
When we execute the preceding search query, it returns a JSON document that
contains the list of documents that contain `Couchbase` in any of the attributes in
the documents. Here, we get two document IDs, which are underlined in red: `2007`
and `201505127`. Now let's fetch the data from Couchbase using the Couchbase web
admin UI; for that navigate to the **Data Buckets** tab. Then click on the **Documents**
button next to the **LearningCouchbase** bucket. In the **document ID field**, paste
`2015051527` and click on the **Lookup Id** button.

You will observe the following result:

A document overview

Congratulations! You have successfully integrated ES with the Couchbase cluster. So, the point of integrating ES with the Couchbase cluster is to enable a full text search in the application developer. An application developer will perform the search query on the ES cluster, extract document IDs from the ES resultset, and use that document ID to fetch documents from the Couchbase cluster.

Using the ES query API

Let's understand some queries used for searching documents in ES. Here is a sample document from the `LearningCouchbase` bucket:

```
{
  "name": "Henry P",
  "book": "Learning Couchbase",
  "skills": [
    "Couchbase",
    "Cassandra",
    "MongoDB"
  ]
}
```

We want to find document IDs for which the user document has the `Couchbase` skillset.

For this, you can query ElasticSearch using the following URL: `http://localhost:9200/learningcouchbase/_search?pretty=true&q=skills:Couchbase`.

If you want to find user documents with the `Couchbase` skillset and name it `Henry`, use `http://localhost:9200/learningcouchbase/_search?pretty=true&q=skills:Couchbase+name:Henry&default_operator=AND`.

```
{
  "took" : 947,
  "timed_out" : false,
  "_shards" : {
    "total" : 5,
    "successful" : 5,
    "failed" : 0
  },
  "hits" : {
    "total" : 1,
    "max_score" : 4.1713552,
    "hits" : [ {
      "_index" : "learningcouchbase",
      "_type" : "couchbaseDocument",
      "_id" : "2007",
      "_score" : 4.1713552,
      "_source":{"meta":{"id":"2007","rev":"2-13de13bcd891ef870000000000000000","flags":0,"expiration":0}}
    } ]
  }
}
```

An ES output

Here, the search criterion is provided using a simple query string as a parameter. And we are searching for all the documents with the preceding criteria in the `learningcouchbase` index only.

These are just the tip of the iceberg. There are a lot of options in ElasticSearch. There are also lots of complex search queries that can be performed using ES DSL. I recommend you to read a book on ES; to get a better understanding about ES DSL.

An API to connect to ES

We have configured ES with the Couchbase cluster and were able to retrieve documents using some simple ES queries. Now let's discuss the steps involved in querying ES using Java APIs.

Here, I am not showing all of the code, as it will become repetitive. You can download the full source code from the website. I am going to show the code relevant to ES and how to retrieve the resultset.

In this process of querying ES and fetching documents, there are two steps. First, we need to connect to ElasticSearch and search the keywords using the REST API. This will return a resultset in a JSON document, as follows:

```
String url="http://localhost:9200/learningcouchbase/_search?pretty=tru
e&q=skills:Couchbase+name:Henry";

static String fetchESQuery(String url) throws Exception {
    HttpGet request = new HttpGet(url);
    HttpClient client = HttpClientBuilder.create().build();
    HttpResponse response = client.execute(request);

 BufferedReader rd = new BufferedReader(new
InputStreamReader(response.getEntity().getContent()));

    StringBuffer result = new StringBuffer();
    String line = "";
    while ((line = rd.readLine()) != null) {
      result.append(line);
    }
    return result.toString();
  }
```

In this method, we passed the ES query as an HTTP URL and used the `HttpClient` library to call the REST API. The result is obtained in a JSON document.

After that, we passed the resultset in the form of a string to the following function. The purpose of this function is to read all document IDs returned by the ES query for the query parameter we passed to ES. We have used the Google `Gson` library to parse the JSON document returned by the ES query:

```
static Collection<String> getDocIDs(String resultStr) throws
JsonProcessingException, IOException {

    byte[] jsonData = resultStr.getBytes();

    //create ObjectMapper instance
    ObjectMapper objectMapper = new ObjectMapper();

    //read JSON like DOM Parser
    JsonNode rootNode = objectMapper.readTree(jsonData);

    JsonNode docListNode = rootNode.path("hits").path("hits");

    List<String>docList = new ArrayList<String>();
```

```
    Iterator<JsonNode> elements = docListNode.elements();
    while(elements.hasNext()){
        JsonNode doc = elements.next().get("_id");
    docList.add(doc.asText());
    }
    return docList;


}
```

Secondly, we parse the result set, the JSON document, and get all document IDs to fetch the actual documents from the Couchbase cluster using the Couchbase SDK Java API:

```
static void boESQuery(Collection<String> dociDs) {
    Cluster cluster = CouchbaseCluster.create("localhost");
    final Bucket  bucket = cluster.openBucket("LearningCouchbase");
    List<JsonDocument> docs = bulkGet(dociDs, bucket);

    Gson gson = new GsonBuilder().create();
    for (JsonDocument doc : docs) {
      Customer cust = gson.fromJson(doc.content().toString(),
Customer.class);
        System.out.println(cust);
    }


}
```

In the preceding method, we connected to the Couchbase cluster and used the `bulkGet()` helper methods to get all the documents for the mentioned document IDs. We used the Gson library to convert from a JSON document to a `Customer` Java object.

Let me provide some insight into the helper method that enables fetching multiple documents using document IDs. It uses the lambda features of Java 8. Using this batch operation, it provides better resource utilization. The `Observable.from()` method accepts collections of document IDs that put in batched for bulk operations, and `flatMap()` is used to fetch documents using the `get()` method and merge the results asynchronously. The `toList()` method enables aggregation of the result with ease:

```
public static List<JsonDocument> bulkGet(final Collection<String>
ids,final Bucket bucket) {
  return Observable
          .from(ids)
          .flatMap(new Func1<String, Observable<JsonDocument>>() {
```

```
public Observable<JsonDocument> call(String id) {
return bucket.async().get(id);
            }
        })
        .toList()
        .toBlocking()
        .single();
}
```

When you execute the main program, the output will be as follows:

```
Name :Henry P, Book :Learning Couchbase , Skills :[Couchbase, Cassandra, MongoDB]
Name :Henry P, Book :Learning OSGI , Skills :[OSGI, TOGAF, Mobile Analytics, Cassandra]
```

The execution'soutput

In this example, what we have done is search for documents with Couchbase in the skills field and Henry in the name field.

Summary

In this chapter, we discussed what full text search is and how to incorporate ES with Couchbase. You understood the various configuration steps of the ES integration. We executed some queries using ES DSL. Finally, we understood how to retrieve information from Couchbase after searching on ES.

In the next chapter, we will discuss replication of data across the cluster using XDCR features for disaster recovery. You will understand how replication occurs in Couchbase—inter-cluster—what its use cases are, and how to monitor it. In addition to XDCR, we will also cover the compaction process of Couchbase.

9
Data Replication and Compaction

In a production environment, we replicate data to multiple systems for the purpose of reporting or disaster recovery. When the source system fails, the replicated data is used to recover the system. Thus, replication provides a way to fail-over the system when there is a disaster. Other than disasters, a replicated system is also often used for the reporting purpose. In order to minimize load on main transaction servers, we can replicate data so that ad hoc reporting queries are executed in the replica system without loading the transaction system. These are very common in crucial transaction systems.

Most database systems provide a mechanism to replicate data between systems through log shipping, mirroring of disks, SAN-to-SAN replication, and so on. Likewise, Couchbase provides a way to replicate documents between systems by buckets. It provides replication, which can be configured in just a few mouse clicks. Replication configuration in Couchbase is very easy, and it can be done through the web admin console. This feature of replicating documents is called Cross Data Center Replication (XDCR) in a Couchbase system.

In this chapter, we will discuss the XDCR features of Couchbase for data replication, which in turn can provide data locality, thus storing documents closer to its users. We will also discuss the need for XDCR and its various use cases. You will learn the various options available for configuring it using the XDCR console. Couchbase provides a way to monitor the progress of replication from the web console.

At the end of the chapter, we will also understand the compaction process. It's nothing to do with XDCR; however, it's an important process that is required for running Couchbase cluster efficiently. When documents are flushed to disk or deleted, the data files get written and updated, which eventually creates gap within the data file, that is, fragmentation. The Couchbase system becomes slow in performance due to fragmentation while performing I/O operations on the data files of bucket. Couchbase provides a mechanism to streamline this fragmentation using the compaction process. You will understand its mechanism, along with various configurations provided by the Couchbase system.

Understanding the XDCR architecture

XDCR provides an efficient way to replicate data across different clusters in the Couchbase system. It can be used to replicate within a Couchbase cluster system or between Couchbase and third-party systems, such as ElasticSearch, which we saw in the previous chapter. It can be used to replicate data from one cluster to another cluster. They can be in different data centers, which are geographically widespread across continents, for example, replication from one data center in Mumbai and another in London for disaster recovery or for data locality. Data locality is a feature in which an application request from a user will be redirected to the nearest Couchbase cluster, which is physically near to the user, to provide better performances.

XDCR replicates data across clusters. Clusters can be located across different data centers, which can be geographically far away from each other, for recovery in the event of a natural disaster. In one cluster, there can be multiple buckets, and we can configure replication on per bucket basis. There can be buckets that are created for ad hoc reporting, and it can be recreated from one of the existing buckets whenever required. We don't want to replicate such ad hoc buckets since it will consume the network bandwidth and it can be recreated any time from existing documents in one of the buckets. In such cases, we can exclude that particular bucket from replication. XDCR also allows to perform unidirectional or bidirectional replication across clusters.

If you are developing an e-commerce application that can be accessed from anywhere across the globe, you can design your application in such a way that a user connecting from Europe fetches its data from the cluster that is located in London and a user connecting from Asia fetches data from the Mumbai data center. For this, you allow bidirectional replication of data, that is, changes in data in the London data center get replicated to the Mumbai data center, and vice versa. Later in the chapter, you will understand its internals and how a conflict is resolved when a document gets updated at the same time in both the clusters when bidirectional replication is enabled.

You can configure to enable read and write from both the clusters as active-active replication to provide data locality to applications. This follows the Couchbase concept of linear scalability — when there is an increase in load, you just add a few more nodes to handle that load linearly.

XDCR is totally different from intracluster replication, in which a document is replicated in a single cluster for high availability of that document.

Let's try to understand the difference between intracluster and intercluster replications.

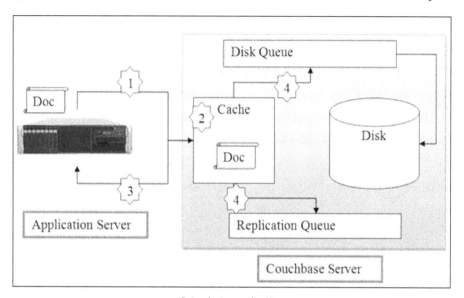

Intracluster replication

In intracluster replication, data that is pushed to the **Replication Queue** number **4** in the preceding diagram is then subsequently replicated to another node in the same cluster. We have already discussed the write operation steps in *Chapter 5, Introducing Client SDK*. In the case of intracluster replication, when a document is written to memory, then it is written to the intracluster replication queue and at the same time added to the disk queue for flushing to the disk.

However, in the case of intercluster replication, there is one more component called **XDCR Queue** that replicates documents to another node in a different cluster, which is shown in the following diagram. All replications are asynchronous to the actual write operation. Once the document is stored in the disk, it gets replicated to the other cluster from the **XDCR Queue**:

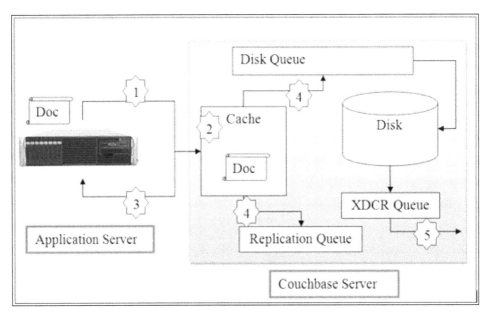

Cross data center replication – the data flow

XDCR pushes all data mutations to replicate to the destination cluster. It creates multiple streams in a round-robin fashion across vBuckets in parallel, which defaults to 32 streams. Whenever there is a network disruption, it will automatically resume from the point of failure. It's designed for resilience to intermittent network failure. Whenever there is an intermittent network failure of the remote cluster, XDCR holds replication and retries every 30 seconds to verify whether the network is available or not. If the network failure is prolonged, then the source cluster will poll every 30 seconds and resume the replication once the connectivity is resumed.

At the time of node addition or removal from the source and destination clusters, Couchbase automatically takes care of balancing the XDCR. You don't need to worry about such issues. If there are multiple writes of the same document, Couchbase de-duplicate it by writing the latest update version to disk and subsequently pushes only the latest version document for XDCR. This is done so that replicated documents are optimized not to consume too much bandwidth. Whenever there are multiple documents with different versions, Couchbase makes sure that it compares the versions to send the latest version of the document for replication.

XDCR provides a lot of flexibility depending on the requirement of your application. You can configure XDCR only for those buckets that require replication to the other cluster selectively. Moreover, you can define unidirectional replication for some buckets and bidirectional replication for some buckets. You can have a mixture of the different types of replication directions.

XDCR supports continuous replication of documents. It doesn't mandate for the cluster to have a certain number of nodes or a configuration. It is adaptable to changes in cluster topologies. When one node is being added or is down, XDCR can understand it and perform the replication seamlessly without any manual intervention.

The replication process is governed by the source cluster or the destination cluster. The source cluster XDCR keeps a track of the mutated documents and maintains a checkpoint to push documents to the destination cluster. If the connectivity between the clusters breaks, the replication will be continued from the previous checkpoint. XDCR is optimized for bandwidth consumption while replicating documents across the cluster, and it also provides eventual consistency across clusters. A bidirectional XDCR is as shown in the following figure:

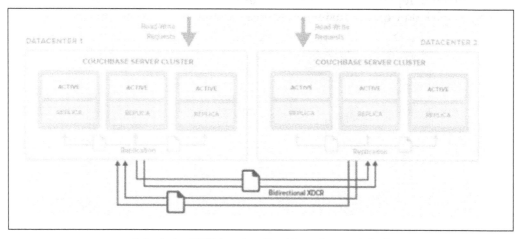

Intercluster XDCR (courtesy Couchbase documentation)

Active-active conflict resolution

We will now talk about the features of XDCR wherein both clusters can be in active-active mode. This means that a document can be mutated in both of them at the same time. Have you ever thought what will happen in this case (cluster A and cluster B configure XDCR bidirectional replication, that is, when a document is updated at the same time in both the cluster A and B)?

Couchbase provides eventual consistency across clusters, and for a conflict like this, it has a built-in conflict resolution mechanism. This mechanism will pick the winner out of the mutated documents, which has the latest timestamp when the same document is mutated in both the clusters simultaneously and replication is active-active between the clusters.

So how does Couchbase decide the winner out of the two (one document mutated on cluster A and the same document mutated on cluster B)? It goes by the metadata of the document. Whenever there is such a conflict, the document that has the latest timestamp and CAS value will be the winner. You can view all the reports of XDCR, which we will discuss in a later section.

Configuration and monitoring

Having understood the concepts of XDCR, let's try to configure XDCR using the admin UI. In order to configure it, we need to log on to the web admin UI and use the XDCR tab. Let's recall what we did in the previous chapter; we configured XDCR in a unidirection replication from a Couchbase cluster to an ElasticSearch cluster. When you click on **Create Cluster Reference**, the following panel will pop up:

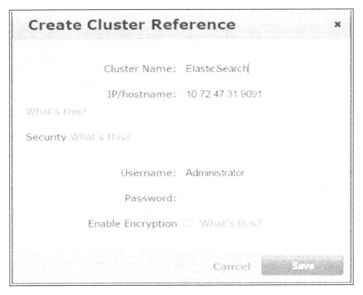

XDCR cluster configuration

You need to enter the name of the cluster; it's just a logical name. You also need to specify the destination cluster hostname/IP in the **IP/hostname** text box. In the security section, you can specify the username and password of the credential to connect to the destination cluster. Then, where is the source cluster? It's the cluster that you connected with the web admin UI.

If you want to enable encryption for the traffic between the clusters while performing the XDCR replication, you can check the **Enable Encryption** box. When you enable encryption, you will be asked to enter the SSL certificate from the remote cluster, which is the **ElasticSearch** cluster in our case.

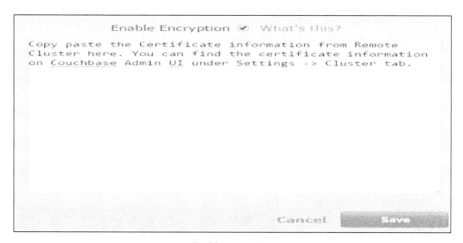

Enable encryption

Once you have saved the configuration using the **Save** button, you will get one entry in the XDCR tab of the admin UI, as shown here:

The remote cluster—XDCR

After you have defined the remote cluster for replication, you will need to specify the bucket and the related settings for the actual replication. For that, click on the **Create Replication** button below the **Remote Clusters** section, and you will see this:

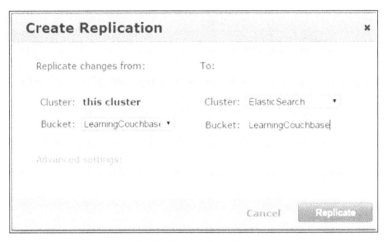

Replication configuration

Replication is configured per bucket; you can select the bucket from the dropdown on the left-hand side of the panel as shown in the preceding screenshot, in which we selected **LearningCouchbase**. On the right-hand side, that is, the **To** column, you can specify the remote cluster that was registered earlier, and enter the bucket name of the remote cluster.

You can specify some advanced setting. For that, click on the **Advanced settings** button, and you will see something like this:

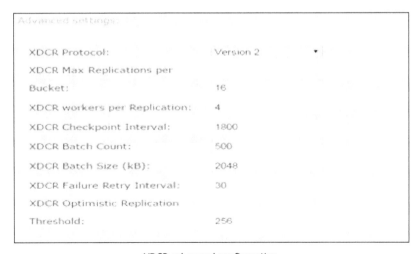

XDCR advanced configuration

You will see a panel for entering the configuration of the XDCR settings. Here, you can specify the protocol version, number of worker processes for replication, batch size, failure retry interval, and so on.

 Most of the time the default setting is recommended, however you can change the setting according to your environment. You can increase the retry interval if the bandwidth between the clusters is slow in nature.

Then, after setting the entire configuration, click on the **Replicate** button.

Ongoing replications overview

After this, you can verify the status from the XDCR console only. You can see in the preceding screenshot that the status shows some errors. It displays the last 10 errors of replication. You can click on the link for more details on the error.

That's it for the configuration of the XDCR setup.

Oh, that was about unidirectional XDCR! What about the bidirectional configuration?

Although XDCR supports bidirectional replication of buckets, replication is unidirectional from one cluster to another cluster. In order to configure bidirectional replication, you will need to configure two separate replication streams.

Let's assume that we would like to configure bidirectional replication between cluster A and cluster B. You can perform the following steps to configure bidirectional replication:

1. You need to create an XDCR replication as mentioned earlier from cluster A to cluster B.
2. Then you need to create an XDCR replication as mentioned earlier from cluster B to cluster A.
3. You can configure advanced settings, such as the number of replicators, batch size, and so on (optional).

There are two ways to replicate documents to a destination cluster in XDCR.

CAPI-mode XDCR

Initially, the only option to replicate in Couchbase clusters was by using the REST protocol. This process is known as CAPI-mode XDCR. In this mode, the source cluster's worker process batched all the updated documents and sent the batch to the destination cluster using the REST interface. On the destination cluster, the REST interface unpacked the batch and sent each update using a single memcached command.

XMEM-mode XDCR

In XMEM-mode, documents are replicated using the memcached protocol, utilizing the efficiency of this protocol. It increases the replication throughput. This mode is called XMEM-mode XDCR. It by passed the REST interface. In this replication mode, documents are push to the destination cluster using the memcached protocol.

We have already seen replication configuration using web UI, now let me show you the CLI option too as shown here.

You can change the replication mode using the `xdcr_replication_mode` parameter, [xmem | capi], as shown in the following code:

```
couchbase-cli xdcr-replicate -c 192.168.27.15:8091 \\
    --settings \\
    --xdcr-replicator=f4eb540d74c43fd3ac6d4b7910c8c78f/default/default \\
    --max-concurrent-reps=30 \\
    --checkpoint-interval=1600 \\
    --xdcr-replication-mode=capi \\
    --failure-restart-interval=30 \\
    --optimistic-replication-threshold=256 \\
    -u Administrator -p root123
```

Let's try to understand how to monitor XDCR after the configuration, which is very important in daily operations for smooth replication and debugging for any issues.

Monitoring ongoing replications

You can monitor the status of an ongoing replication using the XDCR section.
The **ONGOING REPLICATIONS** panel displays the current status, as shown
in this screenshot:

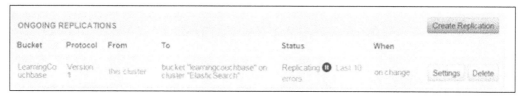

The replication status

The status shown in the preceding screenshot is **Replicating**, which means that
replication is ongoing. You can click on the **Last 10** errors link to view the errors
if there is any issue, as shown here:

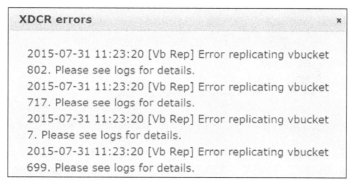

XDCR error details

You can also stop XDCR using the XDCR section of the web admin UI by clicking on
the **Replicating** icon of the status column.

The detailed replication progress

You can view the ongoing progress of the replication from the **Data Buckets** console.

To view it, go to **Data Buckets | LearningCouchbase | Outbound XDCR**, and you will see this:

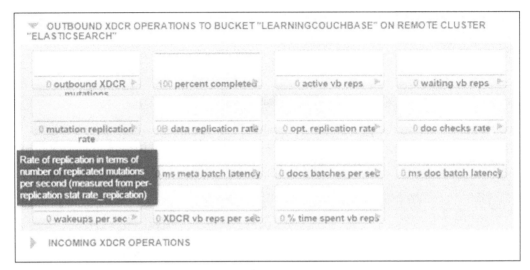

XDCR replication progress

You can hover the mouse over each widget to understand its counter's description.

You can also observe the incoming XDCR operations if it is bidirectional XDCR replication from the **INCOMING XDCR OPERATIONS** sub sections.

XDCR use cases

XDCR can be configured for data locality to improve performance in which data is served from the Couchbase cluster, which is physically closer to the user's location to provide faster data retrieval. It will ensure 24x7x365 data availability even if an entire data center goes down due to some disaster. You can use it to verify code changes in a test environment with the actual production data before moving to the production environment, enabling the developers to test applications on the production data.

XDCR topologies

You can configure XDCR in various ways depending on your application or business needs. Let's understand some of the topologies that XDCR supports.

Unidirectional

In unidirectional topology, documents are replicated in one direction from the source to the remote cluster. It is usually used for read or reporting purposes, offsite backup, development/testing copies, and so on.

Bidirectional

In bidirectional topology, documents are replicated both ways between two clusters, that is, replicated buckets are active in both the clusters. The basic use cases for this topology are disaster recovery and datacenter locality.

XDCR impact

Although XDCR provides various features that enhance or provide much flexibility to your business requirements, there is a price for enabling it in the cluster.

You need to ensure that you perform proper sizing for it, or else there will be performance impact on the existing cluster. XDCR is CPU intensive, and you need to ensure that the parallel stream number is configured based on the capacity of the server CPU. Ideally, you should have one additional core for each bucket configured for XDCR.

XDCR also doubles the I/O usage of the cluster disk. Hence, make sure that you verify the I/O capacity and increase it depending on the IOPS required for your particular application requirements. Besides disk I/O, you will require more RAM for bidirectional XDCR. You can configure an additional 20 percent of the RAM in addition to the capacity required for holding the working data set.

Here ends the discussion on the XDCR feature. Now, let's try to understand another process called compaction in the next section.

Compaction

Compaction is the process of reclaiming disk space and reducing fragmentation. Compaction is performed on buckets as well as on views. Whenever a client deletes documents from a Couchbase bucket, it creates gaps within the data file. If there is no reclamation of this gap, then the size of the data file will increase and it might have an impact on its performance, as Couchbase needs to handle a large file instead of a smaller, compact data file while performing any operation on it. Couchbase works on the principle of append-only storage engine features. Whenever there are data operations taking place in the bucket—whether it's a write, update, or delete operation—the mutated document always goes at the end of the data file only. There might be a lot of gaps between data files if there are lots of deletions occurred. Although this sequential update might improve disk writes, it will have a severe impact if a timely reclamation of the gap is not done. In order to manage the data file's growth, Couchbase periodically makes sure that it cleans up this fragmented space and stale data using the compaction process.

The compaction process

During the compaction process, which is an online activity, Couchbase continues to service the clients' requests. The compaction process creates a new data file, scans all existing data files, and copies all active documents to it, ignoring the stale data. While performing the compaction, there might still be write/update operations occurring in the existing data files. The compactor keep tracks of the delta changes in documents and keeps appending it to the new data file. Finally, when all documents, along with the changes, have been copied to the new data file, it will be used as an original data file until the next compaction cycle, and the old data file is subsequently deleted. Hence, care should be taken that there is enough disk space in the Couchbase cluster nodes, since there will be temporary additional requirement of disk space while the compaction process is running. There might be a spike in the disk I/O while performing this operation.

The same thing happens for the view compaction also. The compaction process will create a new index file, copy the index details to the new file, and delete the old file once all of the information is copied to the new index file. This compaction operation is executed in the background; however, it might impact the performance in terms of increased CPU consumption and disk I/O. Hence, it's recommended to perform this during an off-peak time.

The compaction operation is performed per database/bucket and on a single server. You need to ensure that compaction is performed across the server nodes and databases in a cluster.

The compaction configuration

Auto-compaction, which will compact both the data and the view files by determining the fragmentation level, can be enabled. Where do we specify the auto-compaction configuration?

You can access the global setting for the auto-compaction configuration console from the web UI. Then click on **Settings** and choose the **Auto-Compaction** tab.

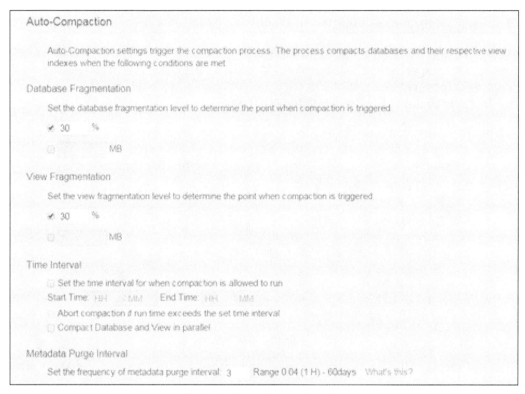

The Auto-Compaction configuration

As shown in the preceding screenshot, you can set the threshold to trigger the compaction process in terms of the database fragmentation level or database fragmentation size in MB. In our case, we have set the fragmentation level of the database and view as 30 percent. This means that the compaction will be triggered as soon as the database or view files cross 30 percent fragmentation. You can also set the same configuration setting for view fragmentation.

Since compaction increases CPU usage and disk I/O, you can schedule the compaction process to happen between certain hours; that is, it can be done in the business lean period. You can perform this configuration in the **Time Interval** section. You can also abort the compaction process if it exceeds the schedule time period by enabling **Abort compaction if run time exceeds the set time interval**. If you have enabled this option and the compaction process crosses the set time interval, it will terminate the entire process.

You can enable **Compact Database and View in parallel** to execute the database and view compaction simultaneously. Otherwise, by default, it executes sequentially.

During the compaction process, you can enable the removal of expired and deleted documents by specifying the intervals in **Metadata Purge Interval**. The allowed range of values is between 0.04 and 60, where 0.04 is equivalent to 1 hour and maximum is 60 days. The default value is 3 days.

Whatever we just discussed can be done at the bucket level as well. For that, you can click on **Data Buckets**. Then click on the arrow icon on the bucket name (**LearningCouchbase**). Next, go to **Edit**. Then click on the checkbox to make the bucket-specific setting as shown here:

Auto-Compaction

Auto-Compaction settings trigger the compaction process. The process comparts databases and their respective view indexes when the following conditions are met.

✓ Override the default autocompaction settings?

The Auto-Compaction settings

This will display all the settings, just as we have done for the cluster's global settings.

You can also perform manual compaction per bucket from the admin console by clicking on the **Compact** button.

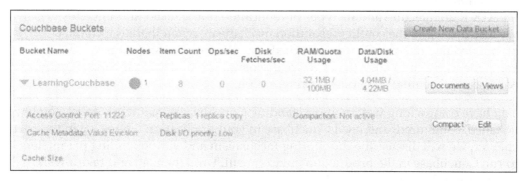

Manual compaction

When you click on the **Compact** button, it will start the compaction process immediately. The compaction status will be shown in the web console like this:

The compaction status

You can execute the compaction command using the CLI as well. The bucket name is specified in the bucket parameter:

```
couchbase-cli bucket-compact -c localhost:8091 -u Administrator -p
root123 --bucket=LearningCouchbase
```

Compaction using CLI

Summary

In this chapter, we discussed XDCR and compaction in detail. You have learned the XDCR architecture and its types of replication (intracluster and intercluster). We also discussed the conflict resolution mechanism; when there is a conflict of mutated documents. Then you learned how to configure and monitor XDCR using the web admin UI. After that, we discussed some XDCR use cases. Finally, we discussed compaction and its configuration.

You have come a long way in understanding Couchbase. Great work done! You have installed, configured, and used Couchbase in your application. I hope so! In the next chapter, we will discuss the monitoring mechanism and various tuning parameters to run Couchbase in the production environment. Until then, go and take a walk. Let your mind gets some relaxation!

10
Administration, Tuning, and Monitoring

In any enterprise system, after its implementation, the administrator needs to carry out lot of administrative tasks for the system to perform well. Administration is an ongoing process. From what I observed in my experience, the most daunting task of an administrator was to make systems run smoothly all the time without any hitch. While managing a system administrator team, I usually advise my team to divide administration into three phases:

- **Rudimentary phase**: In this phase, an administrator has to take care of the basic requirements, such as service availability, disk space, LAN connectivity, and so on. This phase usually consists of monitoring and ensuring that a system is working well and that there are no issues with it. In this phase, there will be a lot of issues, and usually there will be a lot of complaints from the system's users. However, it can be proactively monitored to stabilize the system.

- **Advanced phase**: In this phase, an administrator aims for excellence. It's more of a proactive process, in which the administrator concentrates on performance. They won't be monitoring for availability but for improvement of performance and maintaining a state of the art system. In this phase, they will start applying the best practices in the process.

- **Ultimate phase**: In this phase, everything is automated. There will be minimal human intervention; the system will be running at the ultimate performance with minimum issues. All the activities conform to the best practices and are documented. This phase should be the goal of all administrators.

These phases can be a repetitive process and overlap in phases such as automation. Documentation can be done at the rudimentary phase as well.

In this chapter, I will address the first two phases for maintaining the Couchbase cluster. We will discuss how to monitor, tune, and apply the best practices in a Couchbase cluster. We will also discuss backing up, restoration, and data rebalancing of Couchbase clusters.

Overview

The installation and setting up of a Couchbase cluster involves only a few mouse clicks. It's one of the easiest systems to set up that I have ever seen in the 15 years of my career. However, the job of an administrator is not only to install the system but to also monitor it, verify that it is working well, and take pre-emptive action depending on the current capacity and resource consumption. Administration is a vast topic. It can cover networking, operating system, hardware, and so on. We will be only discussing topics related to the Couchbase system in this chapter.

An administrator needs to ensure that proper backup is taken and schedule for critical database systems. Although a Couchbase cluster maintains multiple copies of documents using replication, there is sometimes a need for backup of databases for critical systems, for audit recommendation or compliance, and so on. Thus, we need to ensure that after taking backup of the system, it can be used to restore the system at the time of a disaster. Periodically, as a practice, we should restore the backup in some servers and verify that everything is working as desired. We will discuss about backups and restoration in the next section.

When the load increases, one of the basic tasks of the administrator is to increase the resources in terms of adding nodes to the cluster. We will discuss how to increase nodes and add resources to the cluster. Often, we need to move existing data to the new database system, Couchbase in our case. With regards to this, we will talk about a mass data loader called the cbdocloader tool. Finally, we will discuss the best practices for designing a cluster and proper sizing to accommodate the data required.

Backup and restoration

One of the regular tasks of an administrator is to take system backups periodically. Whenever there is a disaster, administrators sometimes rely on the backup to restore the data with some data loss, that is, the data that was created after the backup until the disaster or system crash.

Backup is usually of three types:

- **Full backup**: This backs up the whole database. In this, snapshot of the database, the complete current state is taken. Usually, a full backup is scheduled once in a week.

- **Incremental**: This is an incremental backup of the data that has changed since the last backup.

- **Differential**: This is the backup of the transaction that has happened since the last full backup.

cbbackup

Couchbase provides the cbbackup command to take a backup of the Couchbase system. This command enables you to back up an entire cluster, a single node, or a single bucket into a flexible backup structure that allows the restoration of data in the same or different clusters and buckets.

The backup files will be created on disk, and it's recommended to store it in a local disk only. Couchbase takes backups in the SQLite format. This format has some issues while writing to remote file systems. Hence, it's not recommended to direct the output of cbbackup to a remote file system.

Backing up all nodes and all buckets

The following command will initiate a full backup (the -m full option) of all the buckets in the cluster. The backup will be dumped in the D:/mybackup1509 folder:

```
cbbackup -m full http://10.72.47.31:8091 D:/mybackup1509
```

```
D:\Couchbase\bin>cbbackup -m full http://10.72.47.31:8091 D:/mybackup1509
  [##################] 100.0% (8/estimated 8 msgs)
bucket: LearningCouchbase, msgs transferred...
       :                total |          last |      per sec
 byte  :                  920 |           920 |        317.2
  [##################] 100.0% (7303/estimated 7303 msgs)
bucket: beer-sample, msgs transferred...
       :                total |          last |      per sec
 byte  :              2542469 |       2542469 |     441018.0
  [##########################] 150.0% (3/estimated 2 msgs)
bucket: default, msgs transferred...
       :                total |          last |      per sec
 byte  :              2543243 |       2543243 |   1617839.0
done
```

cbbackup – full backup

The preceding diagram displays the progress status when the backup is initiated.

If you want to take a differential backup, change the –m parameter to `diff`, as shown in the following code:

```
cbbackup -m diff http://10.72.47.31:8091 D:/mybackup1509
```

cbbackup – differential backup

When you execute a backup of the cluster using the `cbbackup` tool, it will create a hierarchy of directory structures inside the destination backup folder specified in the backup command.

The first directory level will be a directory with the timestamp as the name of the directory. Beneath it will be a subdirectory with the timestamp appended with `full` or `diff`, depending on the type of backup.

Then there will be a subdirectory for each of the buckets in the cluster, which in turn will have a subdirectory for each of the nodes in the cluster. The backup files for each node of the cluster will be dumped inside the respective node directory, as shown in the following screenshot:

The backup folder

Backing up all nodes for a single bucket

You can also back up a single bucket in the cluster; for example, the following command will backup a single bucket only, that is, it takes a backup of the default bucket:

```
cbbackup couchbase://10.72.47.58:8091 /backup-SN-D -m full -b default
```

Backing up a single node for a single bucket

You can also take a backup of a single node by specifying the single-node parameter, like this:

```
cbbackup couchbase://10.72.47.58:8091 /backup-SN -m diff --single-node
```

Restoring using the cbrestore tool

We have seen how to take backups using the cbbackup tool. Let's now discuss how to restore it if the need arises because of data corruption, for testing, and so on. Couchbase provides a restoration tool called cbrestore to enable the restoration of a bucket from an earlier backup. You need to create the bucket before restoring it in the cluster. When you execute the cbrestore restoration command, you need to specify the backup folder. The following command will restore the backup in the mybackup1509 folder for a single bucket, LearningCouchbase, to a different bucket, LC. You need to ensure that the LC bucket is created before executing this command:

```
cbrestore d:/mybackup1509 http://10.72.47.31:8091 --bucket-
source=LearningCouchbase --bucket-destination=LC -u Administrator -p
root123
```

```
D:\Couchbase\bin>cbrestore d:/mybackup1509 http://10.72.47.31:8091 --bucket-sour
ce=LearningCouchbase --bucket-destination=LC -u Administrator -p root123
  [###############################] 100.0% (8/estimated 8 msgs)
bucket: LearningCouchbase, msgs transferred...
       :                total |          last |      per sec
  byte :                  920 |           920 |       1044.3
done

D:\Couchbase\bin>
```

cbrestore

After you have executed the restoration command, in the web console you can verify that documents in the **LearningCouchbase** bucket have been restored in the **LC** bucket, as shown in the following screenshot:

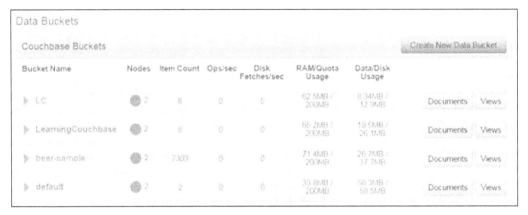

Buckets

Backing up the Couchbase cluster using file copies

You can also backup the Couchbase cluster using the file copies options. You can use cbbackup and specify the directory of the data paths, or use the copy command of the respective operating system. A running or offline cluster can be backed up by copying the data files on each of the nodes.

In Windows, you need to copy the following folder to another location to take a backup of the LearningCouchbase bucket:

`D:\Couchbase\var\lib\couchbase\data\LearningCouchbase`

In Unix, you can execute the copy (cp) command to take a backup of the LC bucket, as shown in this line:

`cp -R /opt/couchbase/var/lib/couchbase/data/LC   /ext/myback-20150827`

You can also use the cbbackup command to perform a file backup of the Couchbase bucket as shown here:

```
cbbackup   couchstore-
files:///opt/couchbase/var/lib/couchbase/data/LC /ext/myback-20150827
```

However, if you use the file copy method to take a backup, you can only restore to a cluster with an identical cluster configuration. You need to ensure that you copy the `config.dat` file from each of the cluster nodes. This is located in the following path for our configuration:

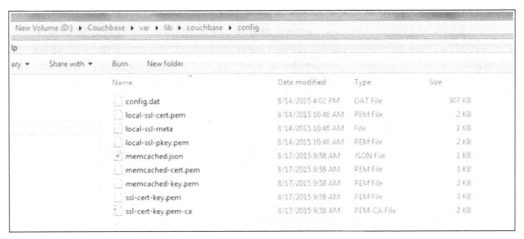

config.dat – the config details

Rebalancing

The process of distributing documents across the nodes in the cluster is called rebalancing.

As an administrators, we need to expand the cluster size by adding nodes to a cluster whenever there are resource constraints due to increases in the application load. Sometimes, we need to trim the resources of the cluster, for example, removing nodes for upgrades of software, hardware maintenance, and so on. Whenever there is a change in cluster resources, the administrator needs to perform balancing of data across the nodes. This is a deliberate process that needs to be done manually by the administrator. In Couchbase, data is distributed across nodes using the vBucket structure. During the rebalancing process, the documents stored in the vBuckets are redistributed among the nodes available at the time of the process to reflect the actual resources of the cluster.

This is an online activity; that is, the Couchbase cluster will be running and serving the clients requests during rebalancing, while data movement occurs in the background. After the rebalancing process, the client needs to be updated about the new data location. This will happen when the vBucket map has been updated automatically to the client, when it polls for the cluster information. We will discuss how to initiate rebalancing in the next section.

Adding and removing a node from the cluster

Your project manager calls you up and asks you to add one node to the cluster to increase the capacity of the cluster. So, what would you do? You need to install the Couchbase server on the new server, and in the installation wizard, you need to ensure that you select the **Join a cluster now** option, as shown in the following screenshot. Then, you need to enter the IP address of the existing cluster (in our case, this is 10.72.47.31) and the login credentials to connect to the cluster:

Joining to the cluster –the configuration

Then click on **Next**. You will be shown the following screen:

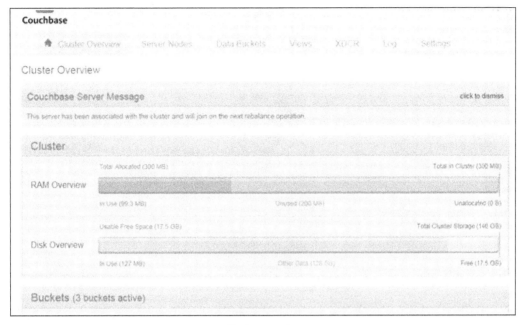

Cluster overview

In the preceding screenshot, the **Couchbase Server Message** sections display that a new node is associated with the cluster and requires rebalancing to distribute data across nodes.

Click on the **Server Nodes** tab and then on **Pending Rebalance**, as shown in this screenshot:

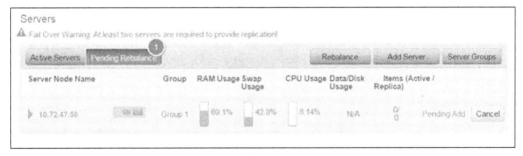

Server nodes

In the admin console, you can see the node that we just added to the cluster. Now, to balance the documents, you can click on **Rebalance**, which is on the right-hand side of the **Pending Rebalance** button. Once you have initiated the rebalancing process, the status will be displayed in the console, as shown here:

Server nodes – the rebalancing status

After the rebalancing process, you can verify the node's status on the console, as shown in this screenshot:

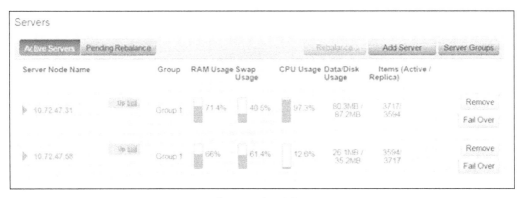

Server nodes status

Performing a bulk set

Often, an administrator needs to upload data to the database from a different system or, at the time of database migration, from one system to another system. Couchbase provides the `cbdocloader` tool to upload a group of JSON documents. These can be a directory or a ZIP file. The following command uploads JSON documents contained in `books.zip` to `LCBucket`:

```
cbdocloader -n localhost:8091 -u Administrator -p root123 -b LCBucket
books.zip
```

Monitoring

Couchbase provides multiple ways to monitor a cluster through the admin web console, the CLI, and the REST API.

You can verify the underlying server processes using the `cbcollect_info` utility. This tool is executed per node and collects information about the overall health of the cluster. The output of the command will be in a `.zip` file. It contains numerous log files. These log files will provide comprehensive information about the cluster:

```
cbcollect_info collect_info.zip
```

```
D:\Couchbase\bin>cbcollect_info collect_info.zip
System information (systeminfo) - OK
Computer system (wmic computersystem) - OK
Computer OS (wmic os) - OK
Service list (wmic service where state="running" GET caption, name, state) - OK
Process list (wmic process) - OK
Process usage (tasklist /V /fo list) - OK
Swap settings (wmic pagefile) - OK
Disk partition (wmic partition) - OK
Disk volumes (wmic volume) - OK
Network configuration (ipconfig /all) - OK
Taking sample 2 after 10.000000 seconds - OK
Network status (netstat -ano) - OK
Network routing table (netstat -rn) - OK
Arp cache (arp -a) - OK
Network Interface Controller (wmic nic) - OK
Network Adapter (wmic nicconfig) - OK
Active network connection (wmic netuse) - OK
Protocols (wmic netprotocol) - OK
Cache memory (wmic memcache) - OK
Physical memory (wmic memphysical) - OK
Physical memory chip info (wmic memorychip) - OK
Local storage devices (wmic logicaldisk) - OK
Checking for server guts in D:\Couchbase\var\lib\couchbase\initargs...
product diag header () - OK
Database directory structure (dir /s "D:\Couchbase\var\lib\couchbase\data") - OK
```

The collect info result

Monitoring startup

Server startup, also known as warmup is a process in which the server loads data from the disk to the RAM before it can handle clients' requests. During this process, Couchbase won't be serving any request from the clients. After the `warmup` process completes, the data is available for clients to read and write. This can take some time, depending on the size of the data. You can monitor the `warmup` process using the following command:

```
cbstats localhost:11210 warmup
```

```
D:\Couchbase\bin>cbstats localhost:11210 warmup
 ep_warmup:                      enabled
 ep_warmup_dups:                 0
 ep_warmup_estimate_time:        358035
 ep_warmup_estimated_key_count:  0
 ep_warmup_estimated_value_count: unknown
 ep_warmup_item_expired:         0
 ep_warmup_key_count:            0
 ep_warmup_keys_time:            29632963
 ep_warmup_min_item_threshold:   100
 ep_warmup_min_memory_threshold: 100
 ep_warmup_oom:                  0
 ep_warmup_state:                done
 ep_warmup_thread:               complete
 ep_warmup_time:                 29633963
 ep_warmup_value_count:          0

D:\Couchbase\bin>
```

The cbstats result

One of the attributes that is worth monitoring is `ep_warmup_state`, which provides the phase in which the `warmup` is currently running in at the start up. It can be one of these states: loading keys, loading access log, and done. Done means the warmup is completed.

Monitoring the disk write queue

Couchbase is a persistent database system that is provided in two phases. In the first phase, it's committed to DRAM. Then, in the second phase, its queued to flush to disk asynchronously. Flush will take place for 250,000 items at a time, until its queue is drained out to the disk.

You can monitor the disk write queue from the admin console.

Click on **Data Buckets** and select the particular bucket that you want to monitor. Select the **DISK QUEUES** statistic, as shown in the following screenshot:

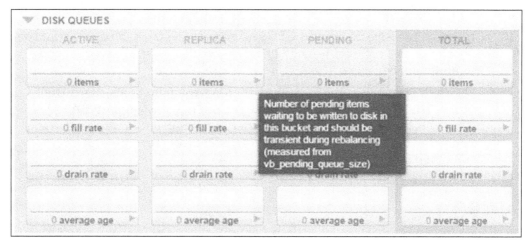

Disk queue stats

You can hover the mouse over the labels to determine the purposes of the counters.

Best practices

Let's understand some best practices and considerations that you, as an administrator, need to keep in mind while configuring a Couchbase cluster.

Cluster design

While designing a Couchbase cluster, we need to think in terms of RAM, CPU cores, the number of nodes, and disk I/O:

- **RAM**: The most crucial component in a Couchbase cluster is the RAM. The optimal response will be provided by the cluster whenever most of the working set data required by applications is located in the RAM. Hence, proper sizing of the RAM is required for good performance. The administrator should calculate the proper working set data and allocate enough memory for storing it to provide optimal performance, since all reads and writes will occur directly through the memory.

- **Nodes and cores**: How many nodes should be there in a cluster? It's better to have more nodes than fewer nodes with high-capacity hardware resources. After calculating the required memory, you can find out the number of nodes required to bring up that capacity. Although the Couchbase server is memory intensive, it requires CPU resources for views, compactions, and so on. Hence, there should be enough cores allocated for it. We recommend a minimum of two cores.

- **Storages**: If there is enough memory for the working set data, **Hard Disk Drive (HDD)** of the **Serial Advanced Technology Attachment (SATA)** type will also be sufficient for the cluster. But if SAS or SSD are used, then you will require less memory. However, SSD disks are more expensive compared to SATA disks.

Sizing

Since the Couchbase cluster is a distributed system, there will be many nodes as part of the cluster. We need to perform proper sizing in terms of the number of nodes and each individual node configuration in terms of CPU and RAM. We also need to consider the network bandwidth for traffic between the nodes, as well as traffic between the cluster and client request.

You can use the following formulas to determine the size for your cluster:

```
no_of_copies = 1 + number_of_replicas
total_metadata  = (documents_num) * (metadata_per_document + ID_size)
* (no_of_copies)
total_dataset = (documents_num) * (value_size) * (no_of_copies)
working_set  = total_dataset * (working_set_percentage)
Cluster RAM quota required = (total_metadata + working_set) * (1 +
headroom) / (high_water_mark)
number of nodes = Cluster RAM quota required / per_node_ram_quota
```

There are some variables used in the calculation of sizing. Their description is as follows:

Variable	Description
documents_num	This is the total number of documents expected in the working set
ID_size	This is the average size of the document IDs
value_size	This is the average size of the values

Variable	Description
`number_of_replicas`	This is the number of copies of the original data to retain
`working_set_percentage`	This is the percentage of your data that you want in the memory
`per_node_ram_quota`	This is the amount of RAM that needs to be contributed by each node to a Couchbase

Variable information – size calculation

Hardware

Any good commodity servers and hardware will be sufficient for a Couchbase cluster. However, some basic requirements for running a cluster smoothly must be noted. Couchbase doesn't require very high CPU usage. However, you can start with four cores for a basic workload, and then add more cores as needed for views and XDCR. You can use drives with a speed of 7,200 or 10,000 rpm. Regarding bandwidth and connectivity, anything that is 1 Gig-E or above will be sufficient for Couchbase. However, there will be benefits if there is an end-to-end connectivity of 10 Gig-E for an application that is particularly latency sensitive or requires extremely high throughput.

Summary

In this chapter, we discussed the various options available for the administration, tuning, and monitoring of a Couchbase cluster. You understood how to use backup and restoration tools. Subsequently, we added a node to the existing cluster and performed rebalancing of data across nodes. In the last section, we discussed some best practices and design considerations to keep in mind while designing a cluster.

WOW! Finally, we have covered most of the features provided by the Couchbase cluster to successfully host a database in a production environment. You understood the architecture, installed it, and configured it. You also learned how to connect to the cluster using the Java API.

We will not be discussing anything new in the next chapter. In it, we will develop an e-commerce application using Java APIs, incorporating all the features you have learned in the last 10 chapters.

11
Case Study – An E-Commerce Application

You have come a long way in understanding the various features provided by the Couchbase cluster. In the first chapter, you understood the concepts of NoSQL and the Couchbase architecture. Subsequently, we talked about how to interact with a Couchbase cluster using the admin web UI, CLI, and so on. Then, we talked about storing information in buckets and how to design documents for NoSQL databases. One of the main fundamentals that you need to keep in mind is to think in terms of denormalizing data. After that, we talked about Java client APIs used to interact with Couchbase to perform CRUD operations and retrieve documents using MapReduce programming, views, and N1QL. We also discussed the integration of ElasticSearch with Couchbase to provide full text search capabilities.

In this chapter, you will learn how to use Couchbase as a database for an e-commerce application. We will discuss some data models that pertain to e-commerce applications and design it then develop a module using the Java SDK. E-commerce is a large application that comprises of various modules, and it's almost impossible to discuss it in a single chapter. We will be discussing only a few models related to e-commerce so as to explain the concepts related to NoSQL and its implementation. However, you can apply the concepts that we are going to discuss in this chapter to implement any business scenario. We will consider a hypothetical e-commerce application so that you can understand the document design and develop a module to place orders.

Overview

Let's suppose that we need to develop an application that will sell books online. We have already decided the technologies to be used for it. We will be using Couchbase as a database and Couchbase Java SDK APIs to develop it. Since we are using Couchbase as the backend, we will be designing our data model in terms of documents. As mentioned earlier, it is impossible to discuss and analyze the entire ecosystem of e-commerce in a single chapter; we will discuss only one or two scenarios.

In any typical e-commerce application, you can browse catalogs, search for products, view them, add them to a shopping cart, and order them. You will have modules for customer registration, inventory management, fulfillment management, advertising management, and so on. However, in this chapter we will discuss only the minimal relevant scenarios so that you understand how to apply a NoSQL document design in the Couchbase cluster.

The conceptual model

Let's implement the catalog and order process scenarios for our e-commerce application. In our use case, we will be selling only books on the portal that we are going to design. However, if the business wants to expand later to include other products, there will be enough flexibility in this design.

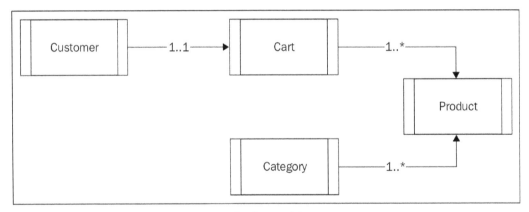

The data model

Our data model is shown in the preceding figure, this is, the database schema. However, in Couchbase, we don't need to create each domain object as a separate entity; the schema of the information goes along with the document. The data model is explained as follows:

- **Customer**: This is a model that a user can browse for a product, which can be bought from our application
- **Cart**: This represents the namespace to group products that a customer wants to buy
- **Product**: This represents books
- **Category**: This groups the books into groups such as programming, databases, and so on

For our use case, a **customer** can have only one **cart**. In it, the **customer** can add multiple **products**. **Products** will be grouped into a category. In our design, a category can have one subcategory.

We will be designing the model to reduce joins as far as possible so that storing and fetching documents is efficient. However, whenever the need to accommodate or provide flexibilities (in order to easily add dependent documents) arises, we will denormalize the information accordingly.

Customer

The following document represents the customer information in the bucket:

```
{
  "name":"Henry P",
  "userName":"henryp",
  "address":{
            "city":"Mumbai",
            "locality":"Goregaon",
            "state":"Maharasthra"
            }
  "documentType":"customer",
  "createdOn":"2015-09-10 10.30.14",
  "updatedOn":"2015-09-10 10.30.14"
}
```

As you can see, it's self explanatory. However, it's worth mentioning the address sub document; we have included `address` as part of the customer information, which in turn allows you to retrieve the address information along with the customer details without any join. If we need to design in an RDBMS, it will be split into two tables, and we will need to perform join operations to fetch address information along with the customer information. What about the document ID? We are using login ID, `henryp` as the document ID, prepending it with customer, for example, `customer::henryp`. As a best practice, we will include an attribute called `documentType` in each document; this signifies what type of information each document represents. Here, we have mentioned `documentType` as a customer signifying that this document represents customer information.

Category is explained in the following section. It contains a `name` attribute, which represents a category `Books`. A category can have multiple subcategories, which in turn can have subcategories. In our design, we have a single document that includes all categories and subcategories. This will allow you to fetch everything in one operation. If you feel that you are going to have lot of categories, you can split it in multiples documents. But then, why do we choose to have a single document? We do so because it will allow us to manage category information easily. However, another school of thought might argue that we should split it into different documents. It all depends on the scenarios. In our case, we are sure that we don't have much categories and it will be modified centrally from one console, so we have gone for a single document structure.

Category/catalog

The following document represents catalog in the bucket:

```
{
  "name":"Books",
   "documentType":"category",
  "subCategory":[
        { "name":"Fiction",
  "subCategory": [ {"name":"Novel"},{"name":"Romance"}]
},
                   { "name":"Information Technology",
              "subCategory": [ {"name":"NoSQL"},{"name":"Programmi
ng"}]
              }
          ]
  }
```

A catalog sample

As usual, we will be using the document ID. The format of the category document ID is `category::books` and the `documentType` attribute is assigned as `category` to signify a category information to differentiate from other documents.

Product

The product or item, which is `book` in our case, is represented as follows.
The document ID is `product::book::1`:

```
{
  "productID":" product::book::1",
  "title":"Learning Couchbase",
  "description": " Design document and implement real world e-commerce applications with Couchbase ",
  "documentType":"book",
  "price":44.65,
```

```
    "img":"lcb.img"
 }
```

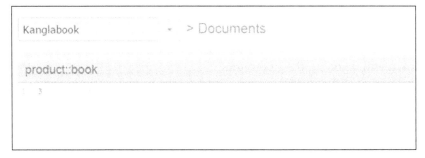

A book sample

In the preceding document, the document ID is a combination of `product::book::` and an incremental value. We have a counter to keep a track of books, which will be increased by `1` whenever a book is added to the bucket.

The book counter is represented in the following screenshot. `product::book` is the document ID of the counter.

Why do we need a book counter? What are its benefits? When we maintain a counter for books, we can determine the number of books without fetching all the books' documents directly from the counter and it is an atomic process. Besides this, we can fetch all the books in the bucket by generating document keys and appending the prefix `product::book::` within the counter ranges. This helps us fetch documents easily from the bucket.

Cart

In a cart, the buyer can add books into it to create an order, which is represented like this:

```
{
"createdAt": "2015-09-16 12:02:50",
 "instructions": "Deliver during day time only",
 "documentType": "order",  "user": "henryp",
"items": [
    '[
      {
        "productID":"product::book::0", "title":"Learning Couchbase",
        "description":"Design document and implement real world e-commerce applications with Couchbase",
        "price":24.65, "img":"cb.img",
        "qty":1, "editable":false
      },
      {
        "productID":"product::book::1", "title":"Learning Couchbase",
        "description":"Design document and implement real world e-commerce applications with Couchbase",
        "price":44.65, "img":"cb.img",
        "qty":2, "editable":false
      }
    ]'
  ]
}
```

Cart

As shown in the preceding screenshot, the cart consists of the user's ID and all the items that the customer has added to buy. The `items` is an array that contains all the details of the products. So, what will be the document ID for the `cart::henryp` document that is prepended with `cart::` to the user ID? We have prepended the user ID along with `cart::` to determine the document ID of the cart. Here, we are assuming that there will be only one cart per user ID.

Order

In the bucket, an order information is represented like this:

```
{
"createdAt": "2015-09-16 12:02:50",
  "instructions": "Deliver during day time only",
  "documentType": "order",  "user": "henryp",
"items": [
    [
    {
        "productID":"product::book::0", "title":"Learning Couchbase",
        "description":"Design document and implement real world e-commerce applications with Couchbase",
        "price":24.65, "img":"cb.img",
        "qty":1, "editable":false
    },
    {
        "productID":"product::book::1", "title":"Learning Couchbase",
        "description":"Design document and implement real world e-commerce applications with Couchbase",
        "price":44.65, "img":"cb.img",
        "qty":2, "editable":false
    }
    ]
  ]
}
```

As shown in the preceding screenshot, the order document is the same as that of the cart. Once the consumer decided to buy the products, the cart is converted into the order. You can include the shipping address, billing address, payment address, delivery descriptions, and so on in the order information as a single document.

An order document

So, what will be the document ID for this order document? Is it `order::henryp::` plus with the current timestamp? We have appended `order::` to the user ID to determine the document ID of the order information. Here, we are assuming that there can be multiple orders for a customer.

We have described all the documents required for our scenarios. Now let's focus on the relationship between these documents. How do you fetch related information? How do we maintain relationships between documents. All of these documents that we have discussed require some relationships among themselves. We will be using an approach to find documents using a reference document. In these approach, documents' relationships are maintained in a separate reference document, and we can navigate from one document to another using the document ID store in the reference document. Using this approach, along with deriving the document ID using counter and the key prefix value combination, we can easily navigate from one document to the related document using the `get()` method.

Why don't we use views to retrieve documents? We can easily do that. However, views fetch documents from disks only. Hence, it impacts performance; we don't want latency in the retrieval process. To provide performance while retrieving documents by client, we try to use the `get()` method for document retrieval, which is the fastest way of retrieving a document from Couchbase. Let me explain the concepts by asking some queries. What are all these queries?

Queries such as these are quite common in an e-commerce application:

- How to get all the products for a category?
- How to get all the orders for a particular customer?
- How to get the cart for a customer?

Let me explain these queries one by one.

Getting all products for a category

Before answering the first query, let me ask you, how do we fetch a category information? Can you determine it? Since, we have only one document representing category, we can fetch using our nomenclature for the category document ID, that is, `category::books`. Once you get the category after a customer has selected a particular subcategory, you can derive the corresponding products that belong to that subcategory using a reference document. This reference document is shown here:

```
product::NoSQL::productList // Document ID
{
    'bookList':[ 'product::book::0','product::book::1']
}
```

We have created a reference document in which the document ID is constructed by mentioning the subcategory in the middle prefix by product and suffix by `productList`; that is, `product::{Sub category}::productList`. The reference document will have an array of document IDs for products that belong to a sub category. In the preceding example, suppose you want to retrieve books related to the NoSQL category. You can use the `get()` method to fetch the document using `product::NoSQL::productList` as a key, and you can again use the following code to fetch the books. In this way, you can avoid using views and retrieve documents faster using a reference document. I would suggest that you use these patterns if you need good performance in your application. Sometimes, you will feel that you are creating an additional document for this, but it's worth creating it. However, you need to maintain some discipline in your coding, such as naming conventions of the document IDs.

The following code demonstrates how to fetch multiple books using the book reference document:

```
public List<Product> findMultipleProducts(final Bucket
theBucket,final JsonArray prodList) throws Exception{
  Gson gson = new GsonBuilder().create();
    List<Product>docList = Observable.from(prodList)
          .map( d ->theBucket.get((String)d)).filter(d -
>d.content() != null).
        map( doc -> (Product)
gson.fromJson(doc.content().toString(),
Product.class)).toList().toBlocking().single();
    return docList;


}
```

In the preceding code, the book ID is passed as a JSON array, which in turn is used to fetch the books from the bucket.

Getting all orders for a particular customer

You need to write a view to get all the orders for a specific customer. The view will be as follows:

- **Design doc**: `dev_orders`
- **View name**: `fetchOrderByCustomer`

```
VIEW CODE

Map

1    function (doc, meta) {
2
3      if(doc.documentType == "order") {
4        emit(meta.id, null);
5      }
6    }
```

The order view

As shown in the preceding screenshot, in this view, we need to select only those documents that are of the type order. Since we are going to search by the order ID, we are emitting key as order id from the view function.

If we want to search an order for a customer say henryp, we can search as follows:

```
http://localhost:8092/Kanglabook/_design/dev_orders/_view/fetchOrderB
yCustomer?stale=false&startkey=%22order::henryp%22&endkey=%22order::h
enryp\u02ad%22
```

```
{
    total_rows: 1,
    rows: [
      {
          id: "order::henryp::2015-09-1612:02:50",
          key: "order::henryp::2015-09-1612:02:50",
          value: null
      }
    ]
}
```

View result

Getting the cart for a customer

The third question is simpler to answer. Any idea? Think about it. You can refer to the cart document, which we discussed earlier to determine it.

Yes, you are right! You can simply append cart:: to the user ID of the customer to create the document ID of a cart, ex. cart::henryp. If there is a cart document for the particular document ID, cart::henryp, it will return a cart document for that customer; otherwise, it will return null. See how easy it is to fetch a document, if we follow some patterns.

What about the inventory? If you wish to maintain an inventory for each book in the bucket, you can create a counter as follows and reduce it as required:

```
Inventory:{productID} // where productID is the product id of each
  document
{
   12
}
```

We have talked about the data model. Now let me show you the process flow of our application, like this:

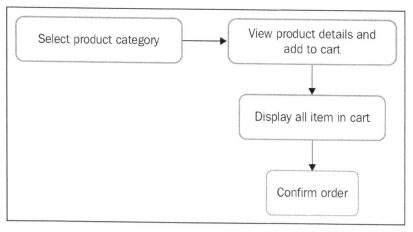

The process flow

As you can see in the preceding diagram, the customer can browse the categories and select any category. The products that pertain to the category will be displayed on the next page. On this page, the customer can add products to the shopping cart. Then the customer can click to view all the items in the cart, and finally confirm the order to complete the order process. The purpose of the application is to demonstrate the document design, so we have not focused on the user interface.

You can download the code of this chapter's program from the Packt Publishing website. We have not included the code in the book due to space constraints. Once you have downloaded the code on your machine, you need to run the maven package to create a war package and deploy the war file on any of the application servers.

Before you execute the application, you need to create a bucket in your Couchbase cluster. You can create a bucket like this:

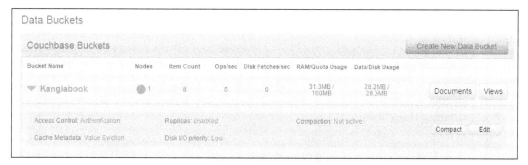

The Kanglabook bucket

You can access the application using `http://localhost:8080/Kanglabook/KBController`

The main page is as shown in the next screenshot, where you need to enter the name of the customer and select the category of the book you want to buy. Click on one of the categories. The next page will display the list of books under that category.

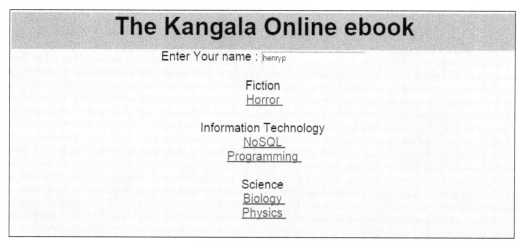

The main page

On the next page, you can add books into the cart, as shown here:

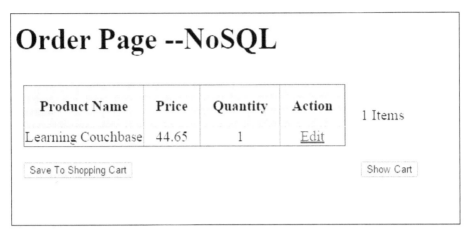

The order page

After specifying the quantity, click on **Add to cart**. Then click on **Show Cart** to view all the books in the cart for the final checkout or to place your order.

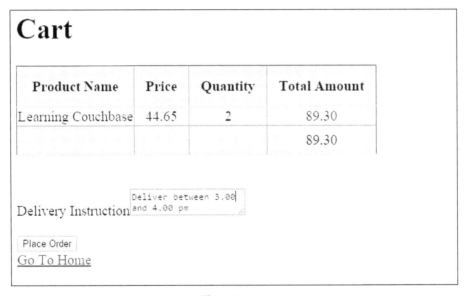

The cart page

You can enter any delivery instruction and then click on **Place Order** to place your order. Then you can verify the order on the web admin console. You can also incorporate views to fetch the details of the order.

Summary

In this chapter, we discussed an e-commerce data model and implemented it using the Java API. Finally, we incorporated many of the concepts we discussed in the earlier chapters. I hope you enjoyed reading this book!

Index

Symbol

3Vs
varieties 104
velocity 104
volume 104

A

ACID
Atomicity 2
Consistency 2
Durability 2
Isolation 2
administrative interface 22
architecture, Couchbase
about 8
cluster management 9
data manager 8
async operations 100
Atomicity, Consistency, Isolation, and Durability. *See* **ACID**
attributes, CouchbaseEnvironment class
computationPoolSize(int) 102
connectTimeout(long) 102
keepAliveInterval(long) 102
queryPort(int) 102
queryTimeout(long) 102
reconnectDelay(Delay) 102
viewTimeout(long) 102
auto-sharding feature 7

B

backup
about 190
differential backup 191
full backup 190
incremental backup 191
best practices, administrator
about 201
cluster design 201
hardware 203
sizing 202
buckets
about 39, 40
Couchbase 29, 41-45
data buckets 27-32
features, viewing 25
Memcached 29, 40
server nodes 26
types 40
built-in reduce functions
about 121
count function 121, 122
stats function 123
sum function 123
bulk set
performing 199

C

CAS 99
cbbackup command
about 191
all buckets, backing up 191, 192
all nodes, backing up 191, 192
all nodes, backing up for single bucket 193
cbrestore tool, used for restoring 193, 194
Couchbase cluster file copies, backing up 194, 195
single node, backing up for single bucket 193

I

indexes
  about 119
  creating 147, 148
  query, explaining 148, 149
insert method signatures 86
internals, Couchbase
  about 53
  ejection 53
  rebalancing 56
  replication 54
  warmup 54

J

Java API
  used, for accessing views 116-119
  used, for querying ES 167-170
Java SDK
  about 85
  CRUD operations, using 85
JSON 59, 60

K

keys 60, 84

L

Lazy Deletion 48
locking
  about 97
  CAS 99
  Lock (GETL) 98
  optimistic 98
  pessimistic 98
Log tab 33

M

map() function 100
MapReduce
  Map program 105
  overview 104-106
  Reduce program 106
  SQL, mapping to 130

Maven

Maven
  about 81
  implementing, for CRUD operations
      with Java SDK 89-97
  URL 81, 90
Memcached
  about 40
  URL 40
metadata, types
  expiration 47
  flags 47
  rev 47

N

N1QL
  configuring 136, 137
  installing 136, 137
  overview 135, 136
  query engine 138
  syntax 140
  using 149, 150
N1QL Developer Preview 3 (NIQL DP3),
      features
  Aggregate 139
  Filter 139
  Having 139
  Join 139
  Order 139
  Select 139
  Skip 139
N1QL syntax
  about 140-143
  conditional expressions and operators 145
  cross-bucket joins 145
  grouping 146, 147
  JOIN clause 144
  sorting 146, 147
node
  adding, to cluster 196-198
  removing, from cluster 196-198
NoSQL
  about 1-6
  availability 5
  benefits 4
  Column family store 4

consistency 5
Document store 4
features 4
Graph store 4
importance 2, 3
Key-value store 4
partition tolerance 5
URL 3

O

observe method 84
ongoing replications
  monitoring 181
operators 145, 146
order information, conceptual model
  representing 212, 213

P

phases, administration
  advanced phase 189
  rudimentary phase 189
  ultimate phase 189

Q

queries, e-commerce application
  cart for customer, obtaining 215-219
  orders for particular customer,
    obtaining 214, 215
  products for category, obtaining 213, 214
query engine, N1QL 138

R

read method signatures 87
read operations
  get (key) 83
  in Couchbase cluster 79-81
rebalancing process 22, 56, 195
reduce method 105
Relational Database Management
  Systems (RDBMS)
  about 2
  versus document 61, 62
replication
  about 54, 55

bucket settings 55
servers settings 55
Replication Queue 173

S

Serial Advanced Technology
  Attachment (SATA) 202
servers 25
Settings option, Cluster tab 34, 35
Software Development Kit (SDK) 22
SQL, mapping to MapReduce
  about 130
  group by clause 131
  order by clause 131
  select conditions 131
  where conditions 131
stale parameters
  about 120
  false value 121
  ok value 120
  update_after value 120

T

TAP protocol 56
topologies, XDCR
  bidirectional 183
  unidirectional 183
touch method signatures 89

U

universally unique identifier (UUID) 69
update method signatures 88
update operations 79, 83
Upsert method signatures 88
use cases, XDCR 182

V

value 84
variables, for sizing calculation
  documents_num 202
  ID_size 202
  number_of_replicas 203
  per_node_ram_quota 203

Thank you for buying
Learning Couchbase

About Packt Publishing

Packt, pronounced 'packed', published its first book, *Mastering phpMyAdmin for Effective MySQL Management*, in April 2004, and subsequently continued to specialize in publishing highly focused books on specific technologies and solutions.

Our books and publications share the experiences of your fellow IT professionals in adapting and customizing today's systems, applications, and frameworks. Our solution-based books give you the knowledge and power to customize the software and technologies you're using to get the job done. Packt books are more specific and less general than the IT books you have seen in the past. Our unique business model allows us to bring you more focused information, giving you more of what you need to know, and less of what you don't.

Packt is a modern yet unique publishing company that focuses on producing quality, cutting-edge books for communities of developers, administrators, and newbies alike. For more information, please visit our website at www.packtpub.com.

About Packt Open Source

In 2010, Packt launched two new brands, Packt Open Source and Packt Enterprise, in order to continue its focus on specialization. This book is part of the Packt Open Source brand, home to books published on software built around open source licenses, and offering information to anybody from advanced developers to budding web designers. The Open Source brand also runs Packt's Open Source Royalty Scheme, by which Packt gives a royalty to each open source project about whose software a book is sold.

Writing for Packt

We welcome all inquiries from people who are interested in authoring. Book proposals should be sent to author@packtpub.com. If your book idea is still at an early stage and you would like to discuss it first before writing a formal book proposal, then please contact us; one of our commissioning editors will get in touch with you.

We're not just looking for published authors; if you have strong technical skills but no writing experience, our experienced editors can help you develop a writing career, or simply get some additional reward for your expertise.

Couchbase Essentials

ISBN: 978-1-78439-449-3   Paperback: 170 pages

Harness the power of Couchbase to build flexible and scalable applications

1. Learn how to install and configure Couchbase Server.

2. Explore Couchbase Servers' extensive key/value API with examples from several popular programming languages.

3. Apply Map/Reduce techniques and patterns to find data in your Couchbase Server documents.

Learning MongoDB [Video]

ISBN: 978-1-78398-392-6   Duration: 03:26 hours

A comprehensive guide to using MongoDB for ultra-fast, fault tolerant management of big data, including advanced data analysis

1. Master MapReduce and the MongoDB aggregation framework for sophisticated manipulation of large sets of data.

2. Manage databases and collections, including backup, recovery, and security.

3. Discover how to secure your data using SSL, both from the client and via programming languages.

Please check **www.PacktPub.com** for information on our titles

R Data Analysis Cookbook

ISBN: 978-1-78398-906-5   Paperback: 342 pages

Over 80 recipes to help you breeze through your data analysis projects using R

1. Analyse data with ready-to-use and customizable recipes.

2. Discover convenient functions to speed-up your work and data files.

3. Demystifies several R packages that seasoned data analysts regularly use.

Infinispan Data Grid Platform Definitive Guide

ISBN: 978-1-78216-997-0   Paperback: 464 pages

Master Infinispan to create scalable and high-performance applications

1. Create highly scalable applications using the Infinispan Data Grid Platform.

2. Maximize your application's performance in any cluster environment.

3. Become an expert in creating powerful solutions using Infinispan through ready-to-use examples.

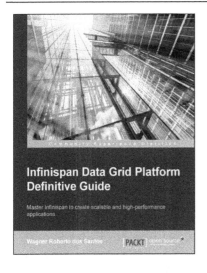

Please check **www.PacktPub.com** for information on our titles

www.ingramcontent.com/pod-product-compliance
Lightning Source LLC
Chambersburg PA
CBHW082117070326
40690CB00049B/3580